Carlo Canepa is a Neurologist who has practised medicine in Peru, Spain and the United Kingdom. He has authored five other books, covering topics such as philosophy applied to neurology, neuroscience and medical humanities. He currently is the Lead for the Neurology Service in James Paget University Hospital.

For my wife, Lorena and our daughter, Valentina:
My who and my how.

Carlo Canepa

NATIONALITY: MEDICINE

A JOURNEY OF MEDICAL DISCOVERY AND PERSONAL IDENTITY

AUSTIN MACAULEY PUBLISHERS™

LONDON • CAMBRIDGE • NEW YORK • SHARJAH

A CIP catalogue record for this title is available from the British Library.

ISBN 9781398438309 (Paperback)
ISBN 9781398438316 (ePub e-book)

www.austinmacauley.com

First Published 2022
Austin Macauley Publishers Ltd®
1 Canada Square
Canary Wharf
London
E14 5AA

I am eternally grateful to my wife Lorena, for guiding me through the emotional hardships that inevitably arise when writing a book like this. Many old wounds and repressed memories resurfaced after many years. She was always aware of how important this book was for me and because of that, never failed to encourage me to continue, even when I was ready to abandon the effort on several occasions. In a very real way, this book only exists because Lorena gave me the strength to get through it.

I owe a great deal of gratitude to my family, in particular to my brother, Marco, for igniting the spark and to my wonderful mother, Patricia, for always guiding me towards that light and reminding me that "medicine is a vocation that requires much more than just scientific knowledge; it requires passion and altruism above all."

And lastly, the admiration and respect I have for my patients is impossible to put into words. They have shaped my life in indescribable ways, making me a better person in the process. In order to fully respect anonymity, I have deliberately changed my patient's names and made sure of not including any personal information that might reveal their identity. Any resemblance is pure coincidence.

Table of Contents

Berkeley

I was born on 18 May 1979, in Berkeley, California. My birth certificate states that my full name is Carlo Silvio Gino Canepa Raggio. Not too American, right? And why on earth three names? Wasn't one enough? Believe me when I tell you that having three names is no fun at all in the second grade! I vividly remember sitting at my desk in Saint Jerome's primary school, just knowing that I'd be called upon sooner rather than later. Why? Well, because on the attendance sheet my name simply stuck out like a sore thumb! It was by far, the longest name on the list of students. Almost every teacher I had, on the first day of class, would take a glance at the list of pupils and immediately get drawn to the enormous name at the top and would say in a rather mocking tone, *"...Who is...Carlo...Silvio...Gino...? Which one is it?"*

I would then slowly stand up and answer, *"All three."* Unfortunately, the interrogatory didn't usually finish there. Oh no, that would have been way too easy. The clincher was if I was asked *'why'?* Try to explain why you have three names (three non-American names might I add) in the middle of a classroom full of eight-year-old boys and girls (emphasis on the latter!) staring at you, some even smirking. And then of course, there was the never-ending name-calling, the horrendous nicknames that chipped away at my self-esteem slowly but steadily. Why couldn't I just have '*one* normal' American name? After all, I had been born in the same place as my teachers and all my classmates!

Time and time again, I was told to 'be proud' of my three names, that I had been given the names of my three grandfathers because I was the first grandchild. Wait, *three?* What? Why? Doesn't everyone just have two? Apparently not. And the confusion grew even deeper when the most inquisitorial of friends would casually ask me on the playground, "Why do you call your grandfather 'Nonno'? Is that some sort of nickname?"

By the time I was roughly eight or nine years of age, one of life's certainties was that my 'Nonno' Silvio and my 'Nonna' Evelyn were my dad's parents. I soon discovered that they had given my dad *only* two names – Raymond Ernest – and not three, like me. I was also aware that my beautiful mum had *only* two names as well: Patricia Carla. I was also certain that her father was my Nonno Gino and that her mother was my Nonna Alice.

My parents and I lived in the quiet, suburban district of El Cerrito, no more than ten minutes away from Silvio and Evelyn (Gino and Alice lived in Lima, Peru). Funnily enough, soon after learning how to speak Spanish, I think at the age of nine or ten, it suddenly dawned on me one day that 'El Cerrito' meant 'the little hill' and that was precisely where my Nonno Silvio's house was: at the very end of Westley Street, on the top of that 'little hill'.

When driving up towards their house, I remember stretching out my neck from the co-pilot's seat, trying to catch a glimpse at my Nonno Silvio's enormous American flag gently waving in front of his house, on the background of a clear blue sky. What a view it was! Standing next to it, he stood proud, puffing at his pipe with the right hand whilst holding on to his cane with the left. As we parked the car, my Nonna Evelyn would always peep through the kitchen drapes, smiling and waving.

Many years before I was born, Nonno Silvio owned a well-known operatic nightclub in downtown San Francisco (on Broadway Street), called the *Bocce Ball*. I was told that it was a fantastic place: live opera singers, great food and drinks. Open till late! It became quite popular. Even the famous teamster Jimmy Hoffa attended one night (I'm not sure if that was helpful for business or not!).

Nonno Silvio's patriotism was his main trademark. He absolutely adored the United States. I guess it was only fitting that he died on a 4th of July. As my dad arrived to Nonno's house that night, he found his body peacefully lying below the flag as a flurry of fireworks silently popped and glimmered over the Golden Gate Bridge.

So, with this background, it makes sense for me to have as a second name Silvio and as a third one, Gino. But what about Carlo? Where does *he* come from? Let me explain.

My maternal grandmother, Alice Olga Dondero Cuneo (1924–1998), was initially married to a man called Carlo Stefano Raggio Cuneo (1901–1957). They were both born and raised in Genova, Italy. Carlo was one of five siblings: Maria Luisa, Giovanni Batista Florindo, Felice Luigi and Rosa Francesca. My Nonno Gino (named after his Gina, his godmother) was one of seven children from the marriage of Rosa Francesca with Giovanni Batista Lorenzo Lavezzo Raggio. Hence, Gino was Carlo's nephew, and actually, he is my mum's cousin! Believe me, it took a long time for me to process that my mum's father was actually her cousin and that my Nonno Gino is actually my *uncle* Gino!

Nonna Alice and Nonno Gino had another daughter, Tania Simonetta. In my younger years, I saw her as an older sister and later, as a second mother. Apart from being my godmother for both my baptism and confirmation, she has also been an example to follow throughout my life.

This is my family. These are the beloved people who I grew up to respect, admire and cherish. My upbringing was a mixture of American, Italian and Peruvian culture. At home, I would hear people speak in English, Spanish, Italian and even Genovese (which is a little-known dialect from Genova). I ate everything from hamburgers, hotdogs and pizza, to ravioli, lasagne, polenta and ceviche, arroz con mariscos and causa. I played basketball, baseball and football as a kid. I listened to opera, rock and roll, Spanish ballades and South American salsa. Essentially, my upbringing was an amazing experience that shaped me for the rest of my life. And for that, I am deeply grateful.

Marco

On Father's Day, 21 June 1987, at 10 am, as I was making my very best effort to listen attentively to the priest's sermon in Saint Jerome's Church, I suddenly felt my right arm being clutched from behind by a massive glove-like hand whilst a deep voice whispered in my ear, "Marco's here." A paralysing chill jolted through my body. I couldn't even turn my head to look at my dad, who was standing right next to me.

Behind us, stood Nonno Silvio, whose facial expression exposed deep concern, the most uncharacteristic appearance for the stoic man we all knew him to be. Something was wrong. I felt it and so did my dad.

About a month before, in that same church, I did my First Communion. Nonno Gino and Nonna Alice had travelled all the way from Lima, Peru, just to take part in this celebration. Unfortunately, I don't have any memories of that day; however, if I just glance over a few well-preserved photos, I'm immediately transported back in time, reliving those moments, and sometimes, if I'm lucky enough, I can even feel the happiness I can't remember.

During childhood, not only are we blissfully naïve to the ephemerality of happiness but we are also equally oblivious to the pain and sadness that a loss can bring. This emotional immaturity shielded me in many ways: I 'couldn't' feel the depth of emotions that my mother, for example, immediately felt when her parents had to depart back to Lima. And I suppose, the hormonal effect of being pregnant didn't help much either. It was a very emotional time, to say the least.

Whilst my dad was taking my grandparents to San Francisco airport for their return flight to Lima, my mum suddenly felt very unsteady and dizzy. To her dismay, she noticed that she was bleeding: an ominous sign, especially as she was only 24 weeks into her pregnancy. By the time my dad was arriving back home, my mum was already in an ambulance, on her way to Alta Bates Hospital in Berkeley. There she would stay until the birth of my brother Marco, only four weeks later.

During the following month, every possible effort was made by the doctors and nurses to keep my mum from going into labour. Alas, despite all efforts, after four gruelling weeks, Marco was born. Thirty minutes later, my arm was being clutched by Nonno Silvio and our lives changed forever.

Marco didn't give any warning that he was coming. My mum said, "I simply couldn't stop him. It was so fast that I didn't even feel pain." He was scooped up by the nurses and taken away, put into a specialised ambulance for critical patients and driven off to Children's Hospital in Oakland, a centre with a specialised neonatal intensive care unit (NICU).

After 24 weeks of carrying this precious child, my mum was suddenly left alone, knowing that her extremely premature child was at a serious risk of dying. She couldn't even hug him. My dad was with me in the church, so she couldn't rely on him for support either. I can't even imagine what it must have felt like for her.

Although she was exhausted, there was no way that she was going to simply stay back in Alta Bates Hospital without seeing him. So, after some convincing, she was taken to Children's Hospital. Upon her arrival to the NICU, she was wheeled over to Marco's incubator, and suddenly, she was eye-to-eye with her new-born son, an extremely frail 28-week-old child. She turned over to my dad and said, "He looks like my father." Immediately after, she fainted. It was simply too much to take in all at once.

It must have been simply heart wrenching for my parents to have to leave the hospital behind, *without* Marco, the following day. On top of that, with all their doubts, concerns, emotions and fears, they still had to try and explain it all to me. I knew what it was I felt: happiness that my brother was finally here but doubt as to why he still couldn't come home with us.

Marco was only 28 weeks old and weighed a mere 1390 grams. He was truly in a critical state. For the next four months, he lived in a small transparent incubator, that usually remained opened, in order for the doctors and nurses to have easy access to him. The NICU in Children's Hospital, in 1987, had two large rows with 20 incubators parallel to each other. He had the most dedicated group of neonatologists and specialist nurses who took care of him as if he was one of their own. For the medical staff, of course, Marco's case was critical but sadly not uncommon. They were accustomed to dealing with these types of cases: that's precisely what gave them the expertise we so admire. However, for my mum and dad, this situation was unprecedented. Each day brought something new and potentially disastrous. One of the most prescient recommendations given to my mum was from one the neonatologist. He said, "Patricia, remember that from now on, this will be like a carousel; there will be good days and there will be bad days. This will not be a steady journey; be happy in the good days and strong in the bad ones." These were wise words, spoken from years of experience. He was absolutely right. The next couple of months were a medical and emotional rollercoaster.

Although my mum was allowed to visit Marco only once a day, after a couple of months, she started to become somewhat of an expert in the meaning of each beeping sound and flashing light coming from the multitude of incubators. The daily monitoring of Marco's heart rate, respiratory rate, pulse, temperature and oxygen saturation became one of Mum's 'fortes'; not only did she learn what each and every one of these numbers represented but she also learned what it implied if one of these numbers suddenly became either 'too high', 'too low', 'too fast' or 'too slow'. Mum recently told me that the medical staff 'was always poking and probing Marco', that she 'didn't understand the majority of what was happening, although she knew it was important and had full trust in the doctors' and that 'everyday was a coin toss, a gamble, a painful test'.

About three weeks after Marco was born, he developed severe sepsis. He was truly on the verge of dying during those days. On the day that he was diagnosed, a nurse stopped my mum before entering the NICU and warned her that she was probably going to be overwhelmed by the state in which Marco was in. More specifically, because the veins in his hands and feet had completely 'collapsed', the doctors were forced to insert an IV line in his scalp, of all places! Furthermore, they had to do a lumbar puncture, i.e., extract some spinal fluid, to see if Marco had meningitis. It was one of the low points of Marco's admission. I can only admire my mum for the strength of enduring such brutally difficult times. Can you imagine seeing your premature child with an IV in his or her scalp whilst being treated for life-threatening sepsis on the verge of death? It must have been one of the most difficult moments of her life. I have no doubt about that. Having said that, if anyone was able to endure that moment, it was my mum. And indeed, she did. Fortunately, with the appropriate antibiotics and supportive treatment, my brother was able to overcome that dreadful state. Only recently did my mum tell me that the first time I told her that I was going to perform a lumbar puncture on a patient, she was suddenly invaded by the terrible memories of those arduous days. It all came roaring back. She told me she felt the 'same fear' as she felt in those moments. That's how strong those memories are for her.

With each passing day, my mum not only grew more and more knowledgeable of Marco's condition but also, inevitably, started to become mindful of how the other children in the NICU were doing. A little boy by the name of Bruno was one of those children. He was one of the most 'senior' residents of the NICU; he had already been there for almost one month before Marco arrived. Bruno's carrousel ride had been a bumpy one. However, after about two and a half months, he finally was reaching the ability to breathe on his own, in other words, without a ventilator. According to my mum, this was a wonderful yet unexpected development. However, one day, as my mum was sitting next to Marco – probably praying and talking to him through the incubator walls – a sudden spike in beeping activity drew my mum's attention to Bruno's incubator. She knew something was wrong. Soon after, a flurry of doctors and nurses came rushing in to attend Bruno, as his incubator lit up and sounded off the multiple alarms. It was his breathing; after only three days of breathing on his own, his lungs could not take it anymore. Sadly, he had to be reintubated and put back on a ventilator.

Bruno's unfortunate setback triggered off an alarm within my mum. She thought, *if this happened to Bruno, who was apparently beating all the odds, what does this mean for Marco? He's just in. His battle has just started and he still has so many hurdles to overcome. Will he be able to survive?* As soon as this gloomy perspective dawned on her, there was no stopping the flood of tears from coming out.

I was there that day. In fact, it was the only day that I was allowed to visit Marco. As I was sitting outside of the NICU with my dad, waiting for permission to see my brother for the first time in my life, suddenly my mum came out with two swollen, red eyes, completely distraught. I didn't move from my seat. In fact, I didn't even ask what had happened. Honestly, I was rather accustomed to seeing tears and hearing bad news.

After a couple of minutes, a very tall doctor, wearing an impressive white turban, came out of the NICU and sat down next to my mum. He would say something that had such a profound effect, that I'm quite confident that it was one of two main reasons why I decided to study medicine. Amazingly, the other reason happened only 30 minutes later.

With the most peaceful demeanour, he pulled up a chair and after about ten seconds of quietness (which in hindsight felt more like 'stillness'), he looked at her straight in the eyes and said, "If you're going to cry for Marco as well as for other children, then you won't make it. Marco needs you to be strong."

It was a serious appeal made with the typical conviction and resolve of a seasoned physician with years of experience. To my wonder, within a matter of seconds, she stopped crying. I was completely mesmerised by the 'special powers' that this man seemed to possess. As I sat there, I thought to myself, *this man made my mum stop crying! I want to do what he does.*

As I grew older, the memory of that day slowly evolved into a deeply meaningful lesson, which I would – as a doctor myself – try to apply to all my patients: empathy must lead the way towards rationality and never the other way around. First, as a young doctor and later on, as a neurologist, I came to understand that simply providing 'rational', black-and-white 'medical facts' to a distraught patient or family member, without previously showing some degree of empathy *makes no sense to the patient*, even if it feels and sounds perfectly logical to the doctor. More so, it can be very misleading and hurtful.

Once my mum was feeling a little bit better, the doctor turned around to me and said, "Ready to go see your brother?" Of course, I was ready!…Or so I thought.

My mum took me by the hand and off I went, into the NICU, to see my brother Marco, who I'd never seen before. The doors opened, and I gently tiptoed up to Marco's incubator, as silently as possible. In the background, I heard the beeping noises my mum had memorised by now, and as I gazed right and left, all I saw was little transparent boxes that looked like miniature spaceships, full of openings, tubes, lights and electronic monitoring devices.

"We're here," my mum said. "Here's your brother." I slowly stretched my neck over the right side of his incubator and saw this little miracle of nature that was Marco. There he was, fighting like champion, all alone in that transparent box. Love and admiration at first sight! *What a hero that little one is*, I thought! His little heart beating away furiously, as if to be drumming off any menace. There was a multitude of miniscule IV lines connected all over his body and a little red light flickering on his foot, indicating the oxygen saturation of his blood.

Soon after this initial introduction, my mum said, "Look around you, Carlo." And to my surprise, I saw all the drawings that I have made for him during the previous weeks at home! Whilst all the other incubators looked like miniature spaceships, Marco's looked like a fan-fair! It was amazing!

One of my drawings for Marco's incubator (which my mum kept for all these years!!)

As I looked back down at Marco, the nurse said, "Do you want to touch him?" Wow! I wasn't expecting that!

"Can I?"

"Yes, of course you can," the nurse replied. So, she unlocked the little round hatchet on the side of his incubator, and almost as if I had been practising for this moment my whole life, I confidently stuck my skinny arm through and made a fist leaving my little finger extended out so that Marco could touch me for the first time. What happened next is the most beautiful memory I have of Marco, the most precious moment I zealously keep and the other reason why I decided to be a doctor. I gently placed the tip of my little finger on his right palm and as his hand reflexively closed, I was spell bounded by the fact that his hand was so small that his grasp did not surround my little finger! At that moment, I knew he would be okay. I just knew that he *had* to be okay.

Suddenly, his heart monitor started to flicker, showing that Marco's heartbeat had started to accelerate. I guess a bit of tachycardia is understandable when two brothers meet for the first time! As I slowly pulled my finger away, his grasp loosened and the heart rate slowed down. "This is your brother," my mum told me. Indeed, that was *my* brother.

On the way home that evening, I felt different. Something had changed deep within me. I had witnessed a man who could heal with words and clinicians who worked together with Mother Nature to fight for his life. At the age of eight, I was very aware that something special was happening, that my brother was in the hands of remarkable people. Later on, in my life, I understood that I could actually be one of those people. That desire never abandoned me. If I could make someone else feel the way I felt that day, then that would be my life mission.

All throughout Marco's NICU admission, we all held on to particular moments that gave us faith and strength. My faithful moment was Marco's grip on my finger. I *knew* that he was going to pull through after that. On the other hand, for my mum, one of those special moments came during her baby-shower, which funnily enough, was thrown while Marco was still in hospital. It was organised by Cindy, a dear friend of my mum, who during the reunion stood up and said, "A child who was born on Father's Day whilst his own father and brother were in church will be just fine." My mum told me that at that moment, she *knew* Marco was going to survive.

Little by little, Marco's body grew stronger and stronger, and eventually, he became capable of breathing and swallowing on his own. His heart rate and respiratory rate settled. Finally, on 17 October 1987, he was finally discharged home! His discharge letter stated the following diagnosis: (1) preterm infant (28 weeks), (2) significant respiratory distress syndrome, (3) retinopathy of prematurity (4) severe bronchopulmonary dysplasia, (5) feeding intolerances, (6) anaemia of prematurity, (7) severe sepsis and (8) metabolic acidosis. At the time, I obviously had no idea of the severity of these problems, but looking at them as a doctor, I can't avoid thinking that it was a sort of medical miracle that Marco not only survived but that he did so without any residual medical problems.

After arriving home, he required oxygen support through nasal specs for a full year. So, essentially, he was hooked up to a very large oxygen tank whilst he was at home, and when going out – which was only at very specific times – he used a different, smaller oxygen tank. Needless to say, although he was home, he was still not out of the woods. Nevertheless, as time went by, little by little, he continued to gain strength, to the point where he acquired all the adequate milestones for his age. It had been a remarkable – no less than miraculous – recovery. I am the father of a beautiful nine-year-old girl – Valentina – and my wife Lorena and I frequently talk about how strenuous and emotionally taxing it must have been for my parents to go through those days. We have difficulties just seeing Valentina cry if she falls down and scrapes herself! I can't imagine what it must have been to see Marco in such a fragile situation without being able to influence it in any way.

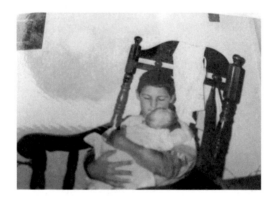

Marco and I (17 October 1987)

I guess that my parent's strength came from a combination of faith, unity and resilience. These are ideals and behaviours that are essential for overcoming any difficulty in life. One day, whilst my mum was sitting and praying with a handful of rosaries, one of the doctors taking care of Marco came over to her and asked her if she was okay.

To this she replies, "Yes, thank you. I'm okay. I have no words to thank all of your efforts to help Marco."

As he pointed to my mum's rosaries he answered, "Thank the one above; I'm only his tool." Although I am not particularly religious – although I do consider myself to be spiritual – I do recognise that having faith in 'something' or 'someone' is essential in these situations. It is a source of resilience and strength. It was precisely the faith my mum and dad had in God, the doctors, the nurses, the people around her, etc., 'as a whole', that enabled them to endure such hardships.

As I look back on those days, I sometimes wonder if Marco would have survived if he had been born in Peru and not in the United States. I especially thought of this whilst I was in medical school and in my internship year, when I rotated through several paediatric and neonatology wards. In 1987, Marco received a treatment called 'surfactant', which helped his lungs develop. In 2003, I was rotating in the NICU of Hospital Loayza, in Lima, and I vividly remember the neonatologist being very excited at the prospect of administering surfactant to a premature child for the 'first time' that day. I had to pause for a moment and think just how lucky Marco had been…indeed, how lucky we all are for having him in our lives.

Another major factor involved in Marco's survival was the financial one. Our human nature tells us that, when faced with a matter of life or death, no expenses should be spared. However, this only applies, if you have the resources. But what if you don't? Well, in the United States, unfortunately, if you don't have health insurance, in all likelihood, you're facing an extremely expensive cost, which is nearly impossible to pay for the vast majority of citizens. My parents, fortunately, had excellent coverage with Blue Shield/Blue Cross Insurance. And because they collectively earned less than $100,000 per year, the government picked up all the extra expenses that the insurance failed to cover. Imagine this: Marco's first day of life, cost $5500! In total, the total cost for Marco's care in hospital was a whopping $500,000 (he used to be called "the half-a-million-dollar baby," as a play-on-words from the popular TV show, *The Six-Million-Dollar Man*, which ran in the US from 1973 to 1978). And remember, this was in 1987. Once again, I ask myself the same question: would he have survived in a third-world country, like Peru?

I will have much to say about the inequalities and injustices amongst different countries' socio-economic and health care systems further along in the book, but for now, let me just state the obvious: Marco would not be with us today if he had been born in a third-world country, like Peru. Poor countries have a very high neonatal death rate, especially when considering premature children. I am confident that a large amount of these deaths could be avoided if these children were born in rich, powerful countries that have the necessary medical resources. This degree of unfairness in the twenty-first century is truly unacceptable.

Marco's birth was the first real, life-changing experience I had. It exposed me to the wide variety of human emotions, stress, anxiety, sadness, happiness, exhilaration, gratitude, forgiveness, admiration, respect, love and so much more. All of these emotions were bundled up into a series of unforgettable and cherishable memories, which have permeated my years as a father, husband and doctor.

Lima

On the morning of 26 December 1980, whilst I was probably rolling around on the kitchen floor, chewing and drooling on my new Christmas toys, in Peru, the citizens of Lima were waking up to a macabre scene: seven dogs, all hanging lifelessly from light-posts, scattered throughout the streets of downtown Lima. One of the dogs, a mutilated black dog, displayed a wooden sign on his chest that read: "Beware, time bomb, may explode at any moment." Lima had been warned. Peru was on standby.

This was the sadistic brainchild of Abimael Guzman Reynoso, the founder and leader of 'Sendero Luminoso' (Shining Path), an incipient terrorist group that had been gaining strength from within the beautiful and historic province of Ayacucho.

As a staunch devotee of Mao Tse Tung (Mao Zedong) – founding father and leader of the 1949 Chinese Revolution – Guzman (aka 'Comrade Gonzalo') during the early '60s, travelled on two separate occasions to the People's Republic, fully embedding himself in the intricacies of the Maoist doctrine. On that infamous day-of-the-dogs, a cryptic glimpse of Sendero's fanatical communist ideology could be read on a shredded piece of cloth, tied on the front leg of another dog, only a couple of streets down, which read:

"Teng Siao Ping, son of a bitch."

Siao Ping, following the death of Mao Tse Tung in 1976, strategically positioned himself as the next 'paramount leader' of the People's Republic of China in 1978, bringing forth a contentious plan (Boluan Fen Zheng) to 'eliminate chaos and return to normal.' In doing so, he directly threatened the political hegemony, generating immediate animosity.

Guzman, on the other side of the world, felt attacked and insulted by Siao Ping's 'Boluan Fen Zheng' and from his own base in Ayacucho would conjure up the attack on Lima on 26 December in commemoration of Mao's birthday, which had been on 26 December, 87 years before.

In 1984, only four years after Sendero's debut on the Peruvian scene, another Marxist-terrorist group by the name MRTA (Revolutionary Movement of Tupac Amaro) also made its appearance. It practised strategic violence, mainly selective assassinations and car-bombings against government, police and military institutions.

Peru in the '80s was submerged in violence, which in turn led to political instability, poverty and corruption. Neither the executive, the judicial or the legislative systems functioned. Whilst selective assassinations of Supreme Court judges annihilated the judicial system, the unrelenting ambushes, hijacking, public murders and car-bombings, not only scared-off foreign investment but also created a profound stagnation in the national growth that wouldn't be overcome for decades.

As it turned out, in 1986, the man who would become my father-in-law almost 25 years later, Coronel Jose Arias Cordoba (better known as Tata), would be deployed on many occasions to Ayacucho, in order to counteract the growing insurgency. He was – and still is – an elite Air Force Commando and as such, particularly well situated to lead this effort.

On one such occasion, he travelled to Uchuracay, a little village within Ayacucho (located at about 4000 metres above the sea level) to kill and/or capture members of Sendero Luminoso. At 4:30 am, a TWIN-212 helicopter led the platoon to a safe zone, touching ground about five kilometres from the objective. After liaising with another military squadron that was already there, they surrounded the village and attacked at 5:20 am. During the exchange, two soldiers unfortunately died and three were severely wounded. But after this intense fire fight, Tata's platoon prevailed and was able to capture nine terrorists and to kill many others.

Once captured, in order to avoid any attempts of escape whilst walking back to the military base, each prisoner was handcuffed to a soldier, with the exception of Marcelino – the most valuable prisoner – who instead was handcuffed to two soldiers. After walking about two kilometres, they reached a large hill with a steep precipice. As they approached a narrow curve, Marcelino suddenly jumped off the precipice, dragging his two captors along with him to their death. He preferred to commit suicide than to give up vital information. Acts of this type not only revealed the unwavering allegiance that was expected from each member of Sendero but also the degree to which the human being can be indoctrinated.

The situation in Peru was dire and yet, in 1989, my mum and dad decided to move the family to Lima. Sounds crazy, doesn't it? Well, in hindsight, it was. To move from a quiet, safe and calm city in the middle of Berkeley, California, to a politically unstable, economically torn, terrorist-infested country like Peru made no sense at all. And to do it with the 'half-a-million-dollar-baby' was even more insane!

After years of thinking about it, I came to the conclusion that the decision had never been based on a direct comparison between the realities or opportunities of two different countries, but that instead, it had been taken in order to prioritise and to protect my mum's mental health and general wellbeing. The year 1987 had left her emotionally exhausted and in desperate need for support from her family. Sadly, neither my dad nor his family could fill the void.

I was also told on many occasions that the move was 'the best decision for Marco'. However, although I believed this when I was ten years old, as a father and as a doctor, I know now that this simply wasn't the case. Marco would have been equally loved in Peru as in the United States. I'm absolutely certain of that. And the medical care he could have been able to access in the United States was simply incomparable to that which was accessible in Peru, especially in the early '90s.

Although I can understand these reasons in the present-day, back in 1989, I was completely clueless. As everyone knows, when you're a young kid, you do what your parents tell you, even if it seems like a bad idea. In those circumstances, you just have to be strong and go with the flow. I knew it wasn't going to be a walk-in-the-park. Just like Marco had had a very rough time on his 'medical carousel', I knew that I was about to start my own turbulent, Limeñan rollercoaster ride.

As with any rollercoaster ride, the beginning is deceptively slow. You are well aware that this is only temporary. Soon after it starts, the tension starts to build as the wagon tilts upwards, starting its steep and bumpy ascent. As you sit there helplessly, you can glance – if you dare to do so – over at the peaceful faces of those below you, safely standing on firm ground, as they look back at you with a hypocritical grin. They are not in your shoes.

Almost immediately after touching down in Lima, my wagon started to tremble: *I didn't speak Spanish.* To my disappointment, apart from my mum, my dad and my Nonno Gino, no one else spoke in English. Only after a few couple of weeks, I was already lacing up my black shoes to attend my new school – Inmaculado Corazon – which was run by nuns, who despite speaking perfect English, insisted that I only speak in Spanish, apparently, in order for me to 'learn'. On my very first day of school, as I slowly walked through the recess yard, trying to avoid eye contact at all costs, I felt how my wagon gradually started to ascend.

Basketball, the sport I loved so much and that my dad had taught me how to play in Nonno Silvio's backyard wasn't popular in Peru. Instead, it was football that commanded all the attention. When it came to food, everything was different as well. I had to eat exotic foods I couldn't even pronounce: aji de gallina, lomo saltado, lentejas, frijoles, causa, arroz con pollo, arroz tapado, papa rellena, bistec apanado, ceviche, etc. Try eating something you can't explain!

The simplest thing, such as watching television, had suddenly become impossible. There was no cable-TV in those days, so every program was in Spanish. Even the cartoons were in Spanish! Watching Charlie Chaplin would have been less painful: at least he didn't speak! Having said this, watching television in those days was a luxury, provided that a terrorist attack hadn't knocked out the power supply to your district, which unfortunately was quite common. Strategic attacks on power plants were routinely conducted by Sendero and MRTA, leading to significant electricity and water shortages throughout the country. In order to cope with this ongoing problem, the city's electricity and water supply had to be rationed. At the end of the week, *The Comercio* – the main newspaper in those days – published the list of districts that would have running water during the following week but no electricity and another list, with the districts that would have electricity but no water. Essentially, you never had both at the same time. I remember how we used to fill up buckets and buckets of water and how we tried to stock up on candles whenever we could. Cold showers with accumulated bucket-water were no fun at all! Neither was trying to do your homework under candlelight. Sometimes, the best thing to do was to simply go to bed and hope that the morning light would wake you up soon.

During those candle-lit nights, if I looked down from my tottering rollercoaster wagon – which was almost reaching the top – I could still see at the distance – albeit, in a much dimmer light – all my friends and family from El Cerrito, still waving in my direction, signalling me to come back down to Earth. The sad thing was that I couldn't. The rollercoaster had already departed, and I was already too high to jump off. Rollercoaster rides are a bit like decision-making: once you're on them, you only have a limited time to change your mind and hop off without injuring yourself. However, if you don't make up your mind fast or if you don't recognise your mistake in time, then it'll be too late, and you'll be stuck in it for the duration, come what may.

Throughout the '90s, my wagon was frequently rattled by unexpected gushes of violent winds, which were incredibly destabilising. Car-bombs, exploding in the not-too-far-distance, sometimes two or even three times a day, frequently hurled emotionally destabilising bursts of air in my direction. One of the most common and terrorising methods of both Sendero and MRTA was the use of TNT-packed cars, vans and trucks, usually detonated in front of hotels, restaurants, police stations, TV channels, embassies, etc., preferably during rush hour. One of those bombs, in fact, the most vicious of all, almost killed my dad. He was only three blocks away from the explosion. Let me explain.

On the morning of Thursday, 16 July 1992, the district of Miraflores became the epicentre of one of the most devastating terrorist attacks ever recorded on Peruvian soil. Two vans, jam-packed with 1000 kg of TNT, exploded at 9:15 am, just outside Banco de Credito, a major bank located on Larco Avenue, the most transited part of the city, instantly killing 25 people and wounding more than 150 others. According to the official records, the blast destroyed 183 homes, 400 businesses and 63 parked cars. That day, my dad was on that very avenue, walking towards the bank, which was due to open at 9:30 am. Had he arrived ten minutes earlier, he would have been killed. That day, my rollercoaster wagon almost derailed.

Following the attack, the first glimpse of redemption came on 12 September, that same year, when Guzman was apprehended and sentenced to life in prison. Although this caused a great sense of relief, we all felt that justice had been only partially served. Even though this psychopath had finally been caged for life, the long trail of innocent deaths could never be undone.

Despite the thousands of deaths, with Guzman locked away for good, Peru could finally start to move on and hopefully start the healing process of so many emotional scars it had borne for such a long time. In fact, there was even more reason to celebrate, because in that same year, Victor Polay Campos, the leader of the MRTA, was also captured and incarcerated.

Alas, despite these major victories in the war against terror, throughout Peru, we continued to evidence attacks of all kinds, coming from the die-hard followers of these two leaders.

On 17 December 1996, the same year I had started medical school, the Japanese Embassy, which was hosting a gathering for a large group of national and international politicians, was taken hostage by a group of MRTA militants. I remember sitting in biochemistry class, which was suddenly interrupted by one of the university administrators, who told us that there had been an 'incident' and that classes were suspended and that we all had to head home immediately. Little did I know that the 'incident' had taken place in the Japanese Embassy, which was located only five minutes away from my house.

My mum, who worked in the Municipality of Lima at the time, had organised another event, almost at the same time for many of the same people who were also invited to the Japanese Embassy. It turned out that those who had decided to attend the municipality gathering *before* going to the Japanese Embassy avoided being taken hostage.

The whole ordeal lasted until 22 April 1997, when a raid operated (Operation Chavin de Huantar) by Peruvian Armed Forces forced their entrance, killing the terrorists and liberating the hostages. I remember sitting in my desk room, at home and suddenly hearing a nonstop flurry of machine-gun shots, firing over and over again, mixed with grenade-like explosions.

After about one week, I walked over to the embassy to see in what state it had been left. As I was reaching it, I saw hundreds of AK-47 shells spread out over the surrounding pavement. I picked up one and kept it as a remembrance of that day. I still have it.

The Miraflores bombing and the embassy incident were just two of the most impactful events in the '90s, but in reality, Peru had been taken hostage for two decades. After the capture of Guzman and the successful raid on the Japanese Embassy, it felt as if the shackles of terrorism had finally been shattered and that the Peruvian people were once again free to dance, eat, work, celebrate and congregate with the peace and the freedom they deserved.

Despite its tumultuous history, Peru has always been a beautiful country. Each one of its 24 departments, each with their own gastronomy, culture, history, rituals and costumes are distributed throughout a multi-coloured geography, showered by a variety of microclimates. Lima is just one of those 24 departments.

A common mistake is to assume that the reality of Lima can be extrapolated equally to the rest of the country. Lima is by no means an accurate reflection of Peru. Decades of centralised government had led to rural vulnerability, which in turn opened the door to political manipulation and to international exploitation. In fact, such neglect enabled opportunists such as Guzman and Polay to indoctrinate those who had lost all hope. Indeed, deserted provinces were the perfect hunting grounds for criminal minds.

Obviously, this untenable situation has led millions of provincials to migrate to the capital, searching for a better life. Who would blame them? Unfortunately, although they had all the right to search for greener pastures, the streets of Lima, contrary to popular belief, were arid and thirsty for solutions. Ironically, the land of milk and honey, of fertile terrain and blue skies are actually, spread out amongst the rural country land, not in Lima.

The only regret I have after leaving Peru is that I didn't take the time to see more of it. Lorena, my wife, on the other hand, has travelled throughout most of it and she always reminds me of the beauties that await me when we return one day. Nevertheless, even if I don't go back anytime soon, I will always have the experiences and the memories of this astonishing country that completely transformed my life.

Lima exposed me to a unique set of social, cultural and political circumstances that were simply non-existent in the United States during those years. Either through newspaper articles, television programs, home conversations or by just walking on the streets, I came into direct contact with poverty, social inequality and corruption, all of which happened on a background of homegrown terrorism. Although no one would ever volunteer to live in such precarious conditions, if it was inevitable to do so, then that person would have the distinct 'opportunity' to unveil those idle virtues that otherwise would likely have remained dormant. In the words of Disraeli, "There's no education like adversity."

Living through such adverse conditions, not only prepared me for life but also sensitised me to the human condition, making me more sympathetic to inequality and more empathetic to suffering. Essentially, it made me a better person and, in the process, laid the foundation for my medical career. Oddly enough, my passion for medicine was propelled by my parent's divorce in 1996, leading the way for many more lessons that not only shaped my life but my career. Not much longer after I lost my family structure, I created my own, which was based on responsibility and discipline. I felt so affected by my parent's decision that unconsciously I thrusted myself full-heartedly into my medical studies, which not only provided me with a safe and reliable refuge but also a road towards emotional independence.

At the same time, I kept thinking what my life would have been like if my brother had not survived and/or if my dad had been killed. Immediately after, I switched gears and thought of all those poor people who instead of just having to 'think' about possible tragic situations, had to *actually live through them* every day. They might have lost a son, a brother or perhaps a dad, to either illness or to violence. Perhaps their dad had been more punctual than my dad arriving to the bank or maybe their brother had been born in Peru instead of the United States. Where was the justice in that? In what type of perverted society was I living in, where, an innocent person, for example, could be killed by an exploding car-bomb or where a premature child – another innocent individual – would most likely die because the hospital lacks the basic technology to keep him or her alive?

All this made me cognisant, like never before, that life was not just about surviving but actually about enjoying your time on Earth, with freedom and health, which are not individual gifts for the few but rather universal rights for all. In the United States, freedom, health care, equality, peace and justice were never under scrutiny, at least at the time when I lived there. In Peru, on the other hand, not a day went by that one of these rights were transgressed on some degree, in some part of the country.

It became obvious to me that human health – both mental and physical – goes hand in hand with social health. They cannot be treated separately, and interestingly, they mirror each other. If you don't care about your neighbour in health, neither will you in sickness. If you don't take care for the most vulnerable people in peacetime, neither will you in conflict.

There are many studies that have proven beyond reasonable doubt that our mental state directly influences our physical one, and of course, the same is true for the opposite situation. Hence, in a society full of anxiety, stress, anger, resentment, fear and apprehension, you can expect a suboptimal state of physical health from its constituents.

All these ideas on life, death, health, social inequality, justice, mental health, etc., little by little became a part of my daily thought process. In some way or another, they were *always* present. And interestingly, I realised that by studying medicine, not only could I place health and disease within a socio-cultural framework but also, I would learn just how influential the latter was on the former.

Essentially, the study of medicine taught me about life in general, which I so desperately sought to understand. And Lima was the perfect setting for me to undertake that challenge. Paraphrasing George Bernard Shaw, during those early years in Lima, "Life for me wasn't so much about finding myself, but rather, about creating myself."

Adriana

Adriana was a beautiful, cheerful and plump six-month-old baby girl, daughter of Luis and Susana, a young couple who had taken a seven-hour journey from Huancavelica to Lima in search of an explanation for the yellowish discoloration that refused to abandon their beloved child since birth.

Huancavelica or 'Wankawilka' in Quechua – meaning 'sacred stone' – is one of the most picturesque provinces in Peru, yet sadly is also one of the poorest. Situated at over twelve thousand feet above sea level and located within a dry, mountainous landscape, it poses unique difficulties for its occupants. The health care, for example, is far from robust and medical technology is as scant as the atmospheric oxygen. The latter, a hallmark of high altitudes, induces the locals to develop a distinctive flushed appearance, a reliable sign of increased haemoglobin (polycythaemia). Adriana had no such rosiness.

'Adri', as her parents called her, was the first patient I was assigned to on my first day as a medical intern (last year of medical school) in Hospital Loayza. To say I was nervous would be an understatement. An icteric six-month-old child is by no means a simple case. I vividly remember glancing slowly over her crib as I tried to remember the most common causes of childhood jaundice. As our eyes met, I noticed her tiny black pupils, besieged by marked yellow scleras. This was not good.

With guidance of the most senior paediatric trainee, we set out a plan to investigate her jaundice. However, I quickly learned that this was easier said than done. Hospital Loazya is a public, government-funded hospital, which means that patients have to pay for their care. The vast majority of patients came from an underprivileged background, many times arriving from the poorest corners of Peru. In certain special conditions, financial aid was available, but this wasn't commonplace. It had taken Adriana's parents a little over one month to scrape together the travel expenses in order to reach the capital. Undoubtedly, they needed all the help they could get. After speaking with the social worker, Luis and I learned that based on the government-funded scheme for patient assistance, they only qualified for a financial relief of no more than 30%. The reason (which to this day still boggles my mind) is because they *owned a TV*. Essentially, only those who were considered to be 'extremely' poor, i.e., not in possession of any sort of electronic device, were eligible for full government funding. On the other hand, those deemed to be 'very' poor, such as Luis and Susana, could only reach a certain threshold of financial assistance. For Adriana's hospitalisation, they would still have to pick up 70% of the total cost. Sadly, under these stringent conditions, many patients – sometimes after days of traveling – simply opted to either self-discharge after a couple of days or to simply walk away from the hospital upon being told they were only 'very' poor and not 'extremely' poor. All this I learned on my first day. I had never spoken to a social worker in my life, much less on behalf of three people who I barely knew. I didn't even know that poverty was 'classifiable', let alone by the bizarre precondition of owning a TV or not.

It was shocking to feel that little Adriana's fate was being determined by the tyranny of harsh numbers and absurd classifications. Not one medical decision had been made yet, and I was already concerned that she would be taken away by her parents in fear of not being able to afford the cost of her admission.

"Can't you cover more than just 30%?" I pleaded.

"I'm sorry," she replied. At that moment, I glanced over to Luis and saw that his pupils were huge, a sign of his overactive sympathetic nervous system, a flight-or-fight response, a true reflection of his inner state. Out of the blue, she lifted her head and said, "What do you do for a living?"

"I sell T-shirts on the street, and my wife doesn't work." That response granted Luis a further reduction in his hospital bill. Because he didn't have a fixed salary, he was eligible for a greater amount of financial relief, which bumped him up to 65%. Although 35% was still a large amount for Luis and Susana to bear, it was a significant improvement, enough for little Adriana to stay.

Even though the entire conversation with the social worker had been a memorable experience, there was one particular piece of information that moved me to the core; I learned that Luis was only 23 years old, *just like me*. As soon as I realised that, I felt deeply embarrassed for the injustice that laid bare. I felt so bad for Luis. As for me, my 23 years of blissful ignorance and painless existence suddenly became apparent for what it *really* was: a stroke of unmerited luck.

What 'special deed' had I accomplished in order *not* to be in Luis's situation, in order *not* to have had his life instead of mine? On the other hand, what had Luis 'failed to do' that was so inexcusable as to sentence him to such an unjust headstart in life? And for that matter, what had Adriana's 'big mistake' been, for her to be at the mercy of such health problems at such an early stage? The answer to these questions, very sadly, is nothing whatsoever. One of life's great injustices is played out at birth, the result of a prenatal lottery over which we have absolutely no control. We're not even conscious of our own existence at the time that life's cards are being dealt. No less than eight to ten years go by before we start to get a sense if life is full of hardships or blessed with comfort. Before then, we are blissfully oblivious and life seems simple, fair and generally equal for everyone. Both Luis and I, as we stood side-by-side in a tug-of-war with the social worker, were painfully aware of who had woken up to a pair of aces and who had not.

Having said this, neither fortunate birth 'rights' nor adverse early on conditions are immutable. They're both equally susceptible to human action or inaction. The former can build upon inborn luck, eventually justifying it and leading to more opportunities, whilst the latter can either extinguish any early on prosperity or lead to greater difficulties than those possibly born with. Luis and I, with our strengths and weaknesses, came out of the social worker's room determined to act together, to tilt the balance in favour of a solution for Adriana, no matter how hard and disheartening the circumstances seemed to be.

I remember feeling invigorated by the outcome with the social worker. I felt like I had really accomplished something important. Little did I know, this was an atypical outcome (a sort of beginner's luck), and that for the next year, this process would repeat itself with almost all my patients, sadly ending with more tears than smiles. Nevertheless, what I didn't know yet couldn't hurt me, so I relished in my success with the naivety of a newbie.

Once I was on the ward again, I concentrated on properly examining Adriana from head to toe. I knew that I was expected to have done this by the evening ward round, which took place at about 4:30 pm, led by the most senior trainee. I soon learned that these afternoon ward rounds were typically not as gruelling as the morning one's but that nevertheless you had to come prepared. I started by listening to her heart and lungs; they seemed normal. I then moved on to palpate her abdomen and found an enlarged liver, which is always alarming, especially in a child with jaundice. Later that day, the senior trainee would point out that she also had an enlarged spleen. In medical jargon, she had hepatosplenomegaly. An abdominal ultrasound the next day would not only confirm our clinical findings but also, very interestingly, showed a very small gallstone in Adriana's bile duct, which fortunately wasn't obstructing it. Although we didn't know what to make of this finding at the time, it would turn out to be an important part of the clinical puzzle.

Her initial blood tests revealed a marked reduction in the number of red blood cells (RBC) circulating in her blood stream, which, amongst other functions, deliver oxygen to the bodily tissues. In an adult, for example, anaemia is usually due to either reduced oral intake or to increased blood loss, seen in, for example, women with prolonged menstrual periods. In the elderly, a new onset of anaemia might reflect an underlying cancer. However, in a six-month-old icteric child, who according to the mother was breastfeeding very well, neither one of these options seemed reasonable. So, we decided to investigate for a rarer cause for reduced RBCs, called 'haemolysis'. In this case, RBCs are 'destroyed' faster than they can be made. RBCs, apart from oxygen, also contain bilirubin. Therefore, if they were being destroyed at a rapid pace, then Adriana's jaundice would have been caused by the bilirubin spilling over into her blood stream. This seemed like the likely chain of events, and therefore, it seemed like a potential explanation.

Soon after, we discovered that her reticulocyte count, i.e., the amount of immature, precursor cells to the more mature, adult RBCs was extremely high, reflecting the desperate intent of her bone marrow to compensate for the rapid destruction of RBCs. Therefore, we had proven that Adriana was extremely anaemic because her RBCs were being destroyed. Medically speaking, she had haemolytic anaemia. The pieces were finally coming together, but we were far from a conclusive diagnosis.

But *why* was all this happening? *Why* were her RBCs being destroyed? This was a very difficult question to answer, especially if you worked in a government-funded hospital, in a third-world country, with tremendous lack of resources. Having said this, as I would soon come to learn and to greatly appreciate was that what hospitals lacked in materials, young doctors compensate with grit and ingenuity. I would learn that nothing focuses the mind quite so well as when looking down the barrel of illness and death. In the face of necessity, human creativity can overcome anything, even if it seems nearly impossible. Doctor Augusto Dextre, one of the foremost diagnosticians in Peruvian medicine, a man whom I would meet later on in my career – in a different hospital – and who would quickly become my personal mentor and idol, told me once – after seeing me struggle with what seemed to be a never-ending stream of neurological admissions and complicated patients – to 'cross my Rhine', which made reference to the unprecedented feat of Julius Caesar's army to build a bridge over the Rhine in 55 B.C., a task seemingly impossible, yet overcome by sheer ingenuity and strength. He used to tell me, "Carlo, a technological dead-end must never entail an intellectual one. If it did, I suspect half of our patients would be dead." These lessons would mark me for life.

And so, our quest to 'cross the Rhine' truly began. After excluding infections and other more common causes of haemolysis, we started to aim our attention towards rare conditions, such as autoimmune diseases, which are due to an unregulated production of antibodies that circulate in the bloodstream, attacking numerous organs, eventually leading to a myriad of dangerous clinical conditions. Perhaps, we thought, Adriana's RBCs were being destroyed by antibodies. In medial terms, this is called autoimmune haemolytic anaemia. Although we knew it was an uncommon cause of childhood anaemia, it seemed like a reasonable suspicion at the time.

In order to understand why autoimmune conditions can cause haemolysis and jaundice, it's crucial to review some basic details regarding the *shape* of the RBCs.

Red blood cells are also called 'Erythrocytes', from the Greek 'erythros' meaning 'red' and 'kytos' meaning 'hollow vessel'. The 'hollow vessel' appearance comes from the biconcave or donut-like shape, which is evident when observed under a microscope. Interestingly, they don't have a nucleus, which provides them with extra space in order to host the haemoglobin molecule. This specific shape is not an evolutionary glitch; it actually facilitates their diffusion through the blood vessels, which in turn guarantees the supply of oxygen to the vital organs. If this special shape is disrupted in any way, then the RBC is no longer capable of flowing smoothly through the blood vessels, and it can literally break, leading to poor oxygenation and to jaundice. Furthermore, the spleen, acting as a natural reservoir for RBCs, will substantially grow in size as the ill-shaped RBCs clog up its tiny vessels, crumbling apart and spilling their content.

So, our rationale was that perhaps some sort of rogue antibody had been latching on to the surface of Adriana's RBCs, destroying them at a rapid pace and leading to splenomegaly and to jaundice. However, our theory quickly crumbled after the 'Coombs test' – an assay that detects antibodies on the surface of the RBCs – was negative. I remember the pressing weight of despair we all felt when reading the result. Where would we go from here? Could it be something even rarer? Had we missed something on the way?

In these very early days of my career, the anecdotes, lessons and life-changing experiences were coming in fast and heavy. One lesson that would certainly serve me for the rest of my career was that when a particular case appears to be outwitting everyone, the best thing to do is to take two steps back and to take a bird's eye view. Sometimes, removing yourself from the tree lets you appreciate the forest better. It felt like a good time to do this.

After conveying on the matter, we all agreed that, although there was no evidence of autoimmunity, the essential problem was most likely still related with a defective RBC-membrane. We knew that autoimmunity was not the only cause for abnormal RBC shapes. It was up to us now to go through the other options with a fine-toothed comb. So, first-things-first: do a peripheral blood smear, in order to directly look at the shape of Adriana's RBCs.

There are several types of abnormal RBC shapes, each one pointing towards a differential diagnosis. For example, if we see under the microscope RBCs with a 'sickle' or reaping-hook-type appearance, then this leads us to a diagnosis of 'sickle-cell anaemia', which is an inherited blood disorder, that typically causes jaundice and splenomegaly by the age of five or six months; as the disease progresses, it can lead to recurrent attacks of pain ('sickle-crisis'), swelling of the hands and feet, bacterial infections, strokes, gallstones, leg ulcers, high blood pressure and kidney disease. If, on the other hand, we find 'sphere-shaped' RBCs under the microscope, then we are facing a diagnosis of 'hereditary spherocytosis', the most common cause of inherited haemolysis in Europe and North America. And yet, a third abnormal shape is the 'ellipsoid', which characterises 'hereditary elliptocytosis', a largely benign condition.

Oddly enough, when looking at Adriana's RBC shapes, they were absolutely normal! Once again, we had been knocked off our diagnostic high horse. The pressure was really on now. Adriana's haemoglobin levels kept dropping to the point of requiring frequent transfusions and both Luis and Susana were growing more desperate with every minute that went by without a diagnosis. And worst of all, from now on, whatever diagnostic test we could come up with was almost certainly not going to be available in Hospital Loayza; hence, we would need to outsource it to a private laboratory, which meant it was going to be extremely expensive. The irony of this case was truly frustrating: no matter how much 'good will' the hospital might have shown towards Luis and Susana, it simply didn't matter at this stage. The obvious lack of medical resources was one of the most heart-breaking downfalls of the Peruvian health system (and it still is). The wealth of intellectual heroism would almost always collide with the tyranny of technological scarcity.

However, much as grit and tenacity emerge to overcome material deficiencies, 'altruism' can conquer poverty. After almost 20 years of practising medicine, I truly believe that the qualities of young doctors reflect the best of what mankind has to offer. If today's money-hungry societies could actually emulate junior doctors' virtues, the world would certainly be in a better place. Once again, we find ourselves facing deep-seated irony: in a world overflowing with material wealth, what it needs the most – *altruism, grit and tenacity* – is not for sale; it simply cannot be bought. What good is an endless supply of capital if it cannot influence mankind's behaviour in a positive way? Before meeting Adriana, I was a naïve young man who thought life's injustices and hardships could be understood simply by reading Victor Frankl, Aldous Huxley, George Orwell or Montesquieu. I had so much to learn and Adriana was quickly becoming my real time instructor.

As her devoted pupil, I went home that evening and read all through the night about every possible RBC problem ever described (at least it felt that way)! By dawn, I felt like a 'hemoglobinologist'! All through the night, I searched for the main causes of 'Coombs-Negative Haemolytic Anaemia', and I quickly noted that the vast majority of causes had already been excluded, with the exception of one particular group of conditions that were exceedingly rare: *enzymatic deficiencies.* Could this be the cause for Adriana's problem? I was so excited at the prospect that I wanted to travel back to the hospital at 4 am just to tell Luis and Susana that I thought I had the answer (even though there was no way of proving it immediately). I would tell him that these were deficiencies in very special chemicals that act as catalysts for crucial biochemical reactions taking place throughout our body and that perhaps, Adriana's RBCs were lacking a specific enzyme. Needless to say, almost immediately after the intellectual high came the economical low: how on earth would Luis and Susana ever pay for this? Such an unsettling problem at 5 am is pure torture.

Two hours later, I was already sitting down with my young colleagues, discussing the details of how we could actually carry out the necessary steps in order to investigate this new diagnostic option. At that very moment, I was learning about altruism, grit and tenacity. I was getting my first true life experience in medicine, brought to me by a six-month-old child. First and foremost: find out if there was a private laboratory in Lima that could actually carry out assays to detect either levels of 'Glucose-6-Phosphate Dehydrogenase' (G6PD) and/or of 'Pyruvate Kinase' (PK), which are essential for the integrity and function of the RBCs membrane. So, after work, on my way home I passed by one of the two specialised private laboratories that I had in mind, and to my surprise, it actually did these tests. As expected, they were very, very expensive and there was no way that the hospital was going to pay for them (although in hindsight, I think it should have). We all felt that they *had* to be done, no matter what. We had come so far; we wouldn't give up now.

Obviously, Luis and Susana couldn't afford it, so it was really up to us – the young and naïve doctors – to do something about it.

And so, we did. The following morning, we all chipped in a certain amount of money, which effectively left us all broke until the next paycheck! Never mind, we were happy to do it. The next day, after work, I took a very chunky envelope full of wrinkled 20 and 50 soles (The 'Sol' or 'Sun' is the Peruvian currency) notes, together with three blood samples to the laboratory. I remember arriving home and falling asleep in the kitchen! I felt that we were really doing something important, something that would profoundly transform someone's life, something that would prove that poverty, injustice and a challenging life were not – should not – be an irreversible dictum. We would turn the tide of Adriana's misfortune.

After a very long three-week wait, we finally had our answer: Adriana had a deficiency in Pyruvate Kinase! This 'enzymopathy' causes problems in the glycolytic pathway, in which glucose (sugar) is converted into pyruvate (pyruvic acid) and hydrogen. The free energy released in this process is used to form adenosine triphosphate (ATP), i.e., high-energy molecules and reduced nicotinamide adenine dinucleotide (NADH). For cells such as RBCs, which lack mitochondria – the powerhouse of the cells, where ATP is generated, fuelling all essential biological activity – the glycolytic pathway is indispensable; it is their only source of ATP; without it, they cannot produce enough energy to maintain normal membrane function. Consequently, potassium and water (and bilirubin) leak from the cell, whilst calcium concentration increases. The cell then becomes very rigid, loses flexibility and is susceptible to being sucked in and destroyed by the spleen, leading to haemolysis.

From a clinical point of view, Adriana's symptoms fit perfectly. The refractory jaundice, the enlarged spleen and even the unexpected gallstones we found on the abdominal ultrasound. PK deficient patients (and in other haemolytic cases) can develop gallstones due to an abnormal accumulation of bilirubin.

PK deficiency is caused by mutations in the PKLR gene (it can also occur as an effect of other blood diseases, such as leukaemia, which we had already ruled out), which is active in the liver and in the RBCs. It's inherited in an autosomal recessive pattern, which means that both copies of the gene in each cell have mutations. Luis and Susana, each one, was a carrier of one mutated gene. Therefore, they had never developed any symptoms.

Awestruck by this diagnosis, I wanted to dig even deeper. Could I prove that Adriana actually had genetic problem? Remember that this was the year 2003 and the accessibility to genetic testing wasn't even close to what it is today. Nevertheless, I spoke with the laboratory who suggested getting in contact with a Swiss laboratory that could most certainly provide further details. After several emails (that *did* exist in 2003!), this laboratory, very kindly, accepted to test Adriana's blood for free! Three months later, we received confirmation of the specific genetic mutation Adriana had in the PKLR gene!

About two weeks after the PK deficiency was confirmed, Adriana underwent a splenectomy (removal of her spleen) and her anaemia and jaundice significantly improved. She grew stronger by the day, and after a two-week period of postop recovery, she was successfully discharged back to Huancavelica. I remember how grateful Luis and Susana were. Although they did not understand the nuts and bolts of their daughter's condition, they did know, however, how dangerous it was and what a blessing it was to finally have a confirmatory diagnosis and treatment.

I never saw them again, and I sincerely hope that that lovely family is doing well. I recall the words of the famous child psychologist and Holocaust survivor Bruno Bettelheim, which resonated so strongly in me following Adriana's case: "Circumstances led me to give up cherished beliefs which had made life comfortable and secure, and to acquire new ones truer to reality."

When all was set and done, I had given Adriana a diagnosis that would change her life forever, and she gave me a life experience that made me a better person.

Jorge

"Help me please! My son is burning."

Those were the gut-wrenching screams that could be heard from outside the paediatric emergency room of Loayza Hospital at about ten o'clock in the morning, on a cold winter day.

The scene was almost unbearable to watch: a screaming toddler slipping through the arms of a frantic mother.

"The boiling water fell on him! My elbow tipped over the pot and it fell all over him. Please help him!"

Little Jorge, this poor 16-month-old child, was on the verge of death. If nothing was done at that very moment, he would die. As we placed a tiny oxygen mask over his face, the nurse tried to put in an intravenous needle, in order to quickly hydrate him. However, this was easier said than done: try finding a good vein in a screaming toddler, covered in third-degree burns whilst his mother is desperately crying in the background, imploring you to 'not let him die'.

Even though his skin nearly disintegrated to the touch, the nurse – who I regard as one of the most skilled nurses I've ever had the pleasure of working with – was able to insert the needle into a tiny vein on the dorsum of this right foot in less than five minutes. She literally saved his life that day.

As all this was going on, I was wondering where he would go after this. In Hospital Loayza, there wasn't a specialised ward for burnt patients and the paediatric ward was not equipped to deal with this specific life-threatening case.

Indeed, as soon as the IV line was secured, I heard the consultant paediatrician ask for an ambulance, to transport Jorge to Children's Hospital (Hospital del Niño), which was about 30 minutes from Loayza. About five minutes later, the ambulance driver phoned to tell us something I thought could only be a cruel joke, yet unbelievably was completely true: 'the ambulance didn't have petrol.'

"What do you mean it doesn't have petrol? How is that possible?" I replied. Apparently, I was told, the hospital administration provided a certain amount of money for petrol that should last one month, yet in this particular month, it hadn't. Hence, in this bizarre world, the petrol tank of the ambulance of one of the biggest hospitals in Lima was empty. And in the meantime, a burning child was dying.

As we all stood there in utter disbelief and embarrassment, I decided to do something that could have well ended my career. "Let's go, I'm taking you," I said. The nurses, the consultant and the other trainees looked at me as if I had lost my mind. Maybe they were right, but to be honest, I probably would have lost it anyways if Jorge died because the ambulance didn't have petrol.

So, I ran to my car, brought it over to the main emergency room entrance and shouted to Jorge's mum to get in quickly! 'We're leaving!'

She sat in the back seat, holding Jorge with one arm and lifting the IV fluids with the other. The screaming was painful to hear. However, I had to focus on driving, on getting Jorge to Children's Hospital as soon as possible. Yet, this wasn't going to be an easy task. Driving in Lima has always been a nightmare and that day was no exception. As soon as I arrived to the main road – Alfonso Ugarte Avenue – one of the most congested streets in the city, I hit a dead end. So, I basically opened my window and started screaming at the cars in front of me to move. At the same time, I opened both back door windows so the people in the cars next to me could hear and see the drama unfolding in the back of my car.

It worked! It got people's attention, and little by little, I started to get through. I even got the attention of a police car, which very fortunately, instead of pulling me over to question me about the bizarre scene going on in the back seat, decided to open up the traffic in front of me by turning his lights on and signalling everyone to move to the side.

So, I pushed through, honking my horn and flickering the front lights like a mad man with his head on fire. As I was swerving through the cars and buses, I suddenly felt a cold chill on my left elbow. I turned around and saw that Jorge's IV line had come out! The saline was dripping all over him and his mum. Essentially, the back seat of my car looked like a murder scene: blood, sweat and tears all over the place. There were even tiny specks of blood splattered over the side window. Despite this, there was no time to stop and fix the problem. I had to keep going.

After about five minutes, we arrived to the front door of Children's Hospital. I parked the car in a prohibited area, picked up Jorge and ran directly to the emergency room, where I was met by a wonderful group of doctors and nurses who had been alerted by my colleagues in Loayza Hospital. By this time, Jorge was very dehydrated, mainly due to the large amount of skin he had lost and to the inability of being adequately rehydrated. His heart rate was through the roof and his blood pressure was very low. In summary, he was profoundly unwell, almost on the verge of multi-organ failure and death.

As soon as he was whisked off to the paediatric ICU, I was left standing there next to his mother, who without saying a word, turned around and gave me big hug. I told her that it was going to take a miracle for Jorge to survive, but that at least we had kick-started the miracle by getting there in one piece! She gave me one more hug and then rushed off to the ICU.

Although I knew that Jorge's chances of survival were extremely narrow, I also knew that he was in the best possible place to beat the odds.

And so, after all this madness, an eerie silence ensued and an odd mixture of satisfaction, angst and hope came over me. I thought to myself: in less than 90 minutes, you met a child on the verge of death, took the senseless decision of driving him across town whilst wholly dismissing the rules of medical correctness and of hospital policy. Was it worth it? Of course, it was. Would I do it again? In a heartbeat.

Few times in my life have I felt so alive. One could argue that the combination of young-age irreverence and naivety is usually very dangerous, but at the same time, it's a wonderful recipe for bravery, which usually isn't a well-thought-out decision but rather a knee-jerk reaction. That day, I felt like I had earned the right to be called a 'doctor', even though I could have lost my licence even before graduating! It's ironic how I 'felt like' a doctor by doing something that could have actually stopped me from being one in the first place.

Reacting without thinking, even though it might sound tremendously irresponsible, especially in a career such as medicine, is something that happens on a daily basis. It's amazing how many life-changing decisions are made in a split-second, without any previous thought process. Those type of seemingly irrational knee-jerk reactions, far from being negligent actions are, in my opinion, indispensable survival instincts and the purest form of human altruism. They are, therefore, 'human' instincts rather than strictly medical ones. And I think that this is the only justification for my actions that day.

Those 90 minutes shaped my life forever. They proved that medicine is not just a series of straightforward, black-and-white cases but instead that it's full of unpredictable grey areas, that put you to the test not just as a medical practitioner but as a human being. For any medical student reading this book, let me tell you that as your career advances, not only will you learn about what you're made of but you'll discover if you're actually willing to rise to the occasion when the time comes. Believe me, you *will know* when that time has arrived. University will test your medical knowledge, but your patients will test your character. *You might think you're a certain type of person, until you encounter a specific type of patient.*

Jorge was such a patient for me. His terrible situation moved me to the core, not only emotionally but also physically. I took a huge risk without even so much as considering the consequences. Certain types of patients have a unique capacity to 'move' you, to knock you off your feet and to fire up your soul, making you do things you wouldn't even consider under any other circumstance. These are the patients that remain in your thoughts and hearts forever. These are the patients who inadvertently 'unveil' the unknown virtues and the hidden defects of their doctors.

I'm pleased to say that Jorge survived! But not before a five-month admission, which included three surgeries, two episodes of sepsis and daily – very painful – treatment for his burns. Treating his pain, I was told, was the most difficult aspect during all of his time in hospital. How do you know if the pain medication is sufficient in a 16-month-old child or even if it's moderately effective? How do you know if his discomfort is due to pain or to something else? It must have been tremendously challenging. Nevertheless, despite all these obstacles, he actually made it. What a strong soul!

I have nothing but praise and respect for the all the nurses, general surgeons, paediatricians, ICU doctors, junior doctors, microbiologists, plastic surgeons, therapists, nutritionists, emergency medicine staff and of course for Jorge's mother, who never lost her faith in Jorge's resilience. As I said before, I might have kick-started the process, but if it hadn't been for the monumental efforts of everyone else, Jorge simply wouldn't have survived.

This is a wonderful example of how the medical care of 'just one' human being can bring together – as it should – a large multidisciplinary team, in which each and every one of its members is equally important. Much as it takes a village to 'raise' a child, it takes a large medical team to 'cure' a human being, young or old.

In the medical world, it is the patient who's at the very core of our lives. The needs of a patient have the unique power to attract many medical practitioners with different specialities *all at the same time*, unifying them under a shared purpose. This medical village, when working together, can accomplish wonderful things for other human beings. That is the quintessential purpose of any medical practitioner.

For the medical students and the junior doctors reading this book, always remind yourselves that when things get really tough, maybe to the point of wanting to give up – which is an idea that crosses every doctor's mind at some point in their career (no matter what people might tell you) – that you entered this profession not for personal glory but in reality, to put yourselves at the service of your fellow neighbour in need, which is by far the highest purpose in life and as such, it will be difficult and will require a great deal of sacrifice. However, I can guarantee you that it's completely worth it. All of it.

Renato

"This is a 34-year-old male patient, who suffered two generalised seizures whilst traveling on public transport. Blood pressure is 175/98, heart rate is 102, respiratory rate is 27, blood sugar is normal and oxygen saturation is 98%."

Whilst the paramedic conveyed this information to the medical team on call, I tried to assess the patient's state of consciousness. "Renato! Can you hear me? Can you open your eyes, please? Can you lift your arms for me?" No response at all, just an irregular and meaningless wobbling of his head side-to-side. As I lifted both of his eyelids, I noticed that both pupils were very small – 'pinpoint', in medical jargon: possibly, due to the diazepam he received on the way over to the hospital. His trousers were drenched in urine and sweat, and his limbs flailed hopelessly.

We were witnessing Renato's 'post-ictal state': the seizures' epilogue, in which, the brain and the body plunge into a semi-comatose state, as if waving a white flag of surrender.

Little by little, he started to regain consciousness; however, he was completely oblivious to the whole episode. He gathered he was in a hospital because of all the patients around him in the emergency department but had absolutely no clue as to why. Disorientation, amnesia and sometimes even agitation commonly occur as the post-ictal stage fades.

By the following morning, not only was he fully awake and alert but he was talkative and eager to explore why this had happened to him. As a first-year neurology trainee, I wasn't too confident in speculating about the diagnostic options at such an early stage in his condition. I think Renato sensed my hesitation and so, rather generously, decided to open up about his private life, as if to break the ice and to pretend, at least for the time being, that 'nothing had happened'.

"I'm an electrical engineer by trade and I love building plane models in my spare time. Unfortunately, I've been out of work for the past six months and yesterday, before all this happened, I was on my way to a job interview." He went on to say, "I consider myself a very healthy person; I don't take any sort of medications and love playing football. I can't explain why this has happened to me." As I was listening to this, it struck me that he was a fearless and clever man, who appeared to be fully invested not only in solving his problem but also understanding why this had happened to him.

As a young physician (and still to this day), whenever the rare occasion came along in which a patient like Renato, who was assertive, open-minded, academic and resilient appeared, I immediately felt excited at the prospect of *learning something from him.* I knew that if I spoke to him every day, if I asked the right questions and if I examined him meticulously, it wouldn't be long before I would have learned more from him than from reading any book on the matter. And so, I set out to do exactly that.

Unfortunately, as expected, he wasn't able to give me too many details regarding the actual attack; however, he did recall feeling more anxious and temperamental during the last two months, something completely out of character for him. His wife, Vanessa, who was sitting next to him, quickly added that she too had noticed a 'change in his personality', with a tendency to become verbally abusive and angry over futile matters. She had also noted that even though he had always been very sharp and focused, lately, he seemed to be more hesitant and lacking in confidence for decision-making. All this struck me as interesting, but I still didn't know if it had anything to do with Renato's underlying problem. Was it just a curious red herring or was it a crucial piece of the puzzle? Even though it was too early to say, it seemed like a good idea not to dismiss it quite yet.

I then asked him to lie down so that I could examine him. After seeing him walk to the toilet and back, sit on the edge of his bed without tilting over, gesticulate appropriately, speak whilst focusing on my eyes and demonstrate adequate comprehension by answering correctly all my questions, I had already 'assessed' the majority of his neurological functions, such as strength, balance, language and cognition. 'Observing' – not just passively watching – a patient when he or she is unaware of it is one of the most powerful diagnostic tools a neurologist has.

Observing, for example, how he could walk unaided and then sit down without falling over, told me that his cerebellum – the organ that controls balance – was intact and that his overall strength was preserved. Listening to him elaborate on a myriad of topics whilst answering my questions appropriately, told me that the 'language centres' were working appropriately. Watching him gesticulate back and forth, told me that not only did he have normal strength and coordination but also that he was able to combine speech with movement. Listening to his multiple childhood memories indicated that his memory was intact. And finally, the fact that he could focus on my eyes whilst talking, indicated that there was no obvious visual loss nor inattention.

Despite all these reassuring findings, I proceeded to examine him anyways from head to toe, and I was pleased not to find any obvious deficits. However, rather curiously, despite asking him to keep quiet during the examination, he continued to talk, almost incessantly, as if it was beyond his control, fleeting from one topic to another. At times, his eyes would swell up in tears, whilst at others he would chuckle like a mischievous adolescent. None of what he said was incoherent; it was just a constant flux of ideas without any logical sequence. It was as if he was plucking topics out of the sky and quickly discarding them. He quickly swung from famous football players to violin virtuosos, from good friends to terrible restaurants and from electrical engineering to holiday destinations. By the end of the examination, it was *me* who was exhausted!

It was striking to witness, 'in vivo', this fugue of ideas, especially because I too have experienced – and still do – the same uncontrollable cascade of thoughts. For me, it feels like I'm riding on a chariot led by six hyperactive racehorses, each one running off in a different direction, and although I hold the reins to these fuguing animals, I have no control over them whatsoever. Their eventual exhaustion is my only hope at regaining control. Not infrequently, this fugue of ideas is associated with a superposition of ideas, a rapid firing of parallel thoughts, analogies and metaphors and visualisation of farfetched 'similarities', such as, for example, seeing the 'H' logo for Honda as a thyroid gland, 'seeing' the 'Google Maps' logo as the periaqueductal grey matter in the midbrain; thinking that I'm driving on the short arm of the G immunoglobulin or perhaps seeing Goethe's opposing colour circle as I see a blue skyline in my rear-view mirror whilst facing the sunset. All this goes on, whilst *Carmina Burana's finale* hands over the baton to Pavarotti's *Nesum Dorma*. Essentially, it's a painfully beautiful experience, at least for me.

Although I deeply empathised with Renato's rambling spiel, at the same time I felt strangely identified with him. As I listened to him, it felt like 'my mind' was on a loudspeaker, listening to my own thoughts being played out on fast-forward mode, right in front of me. It was a chilling moment. It stopped me in my tracks. Could I have what he does? Was this a disease or just a peculiarity?

After a couple of days, we were finally able to arrange for a brain CT scan, which revealed a tumour-like growth located in the left orbital frontal cortex (OFC), one of the most – if not *the* most – specialised parts of the brain, responsible for some of the most sophisticated brain functions, such as, decision-making, social behaviour, feeling empathy, encoding contingencies in a flexible manner, emotional appraisal, inhibiting responses, prediction, planning (forethought), goal-directed behaviour and evaluated reward, amongst others. Furthermore, the posterior portion of the OFC is directly connected to the amygdala (component of the limbic system), which, in turn, is reciprocally connected to the hippocampus and to the primary auditory cortex. The amygdala is primarily involved in feeling pleasure, processing memory, decision-making and emotional learning. The hippocampus, on the other hand, is primarily involved in memory; typically, it malfunctions in patients who have Alzheimer's disease.

Renato's lesion was about 3 x 2 cm, and it was surrounded by a significant amount of water, which was creating mild shift of the surrounding tissue. It appeared as a very bright white sphere, with small black dots in the middle, giving the appearance of a poked-out golf ball. The surrounding water spread out centrifugally, coursing through the axons, much as a river's serpentine streams.

With this information, we could start to put the pieces together. It turned out that the behavioural change wasn't just a red herring but *the* essential and *only* clinical link to the damaged OFC. The involvement of the OFC and of no other brain region clearly explained why Renato didn't have any other – more obvious – physical signs, such as weakness, incoordination or speech disturbance.

Renato's diagnosis reminded me of the famous case of Phineas Gage, a 25-year-old American railroad construction foreman who on 13 September 1848 miraculously survived a hot iron rod being accidentally thrusted through his left frontal lobe, damaging the OFC without involving other areas. Because of this selective involvement, he was able to retain his speech, motor and memory functions – which depend on other regions within the frontal cortex and temporal lobes, respectively – however, his behaviour drastically changed. Soon after his recovery, his treating physician, Dr John Martyn Harlow, described him as follows:

"[Phineas] remembers passing and past events correctly, as well before as since the injury. Intellectual manifestations feeble, being exceedingly capricious and childish, but with a will as indomitable as ever, is particularly obstinate, will not yield to restraint when it conflicts with his desires...He is fitful, irreverent, indulging at times in the grossest profanity (which was not previously the custom), manifesting but little deference for his fellows...His mind was radically changed, so decidedly that his friends and acquaintances said he was 'no longer Gage'."

Renato's tumour was mirroring Gage's symptoms. As a first-year neurology trainee (or resident), that was simply fascinating to me. It felt like I had my own, modern-day Phineas Gage, right in front of me.

Given his open-mindedness and good will, I decided to undertake my own little research project. Late one evening, after finishing my work, without previous warning, I went over to his bed and handed him a piece of paper and a pencil and asked him to draw anything he wanted during the next 20 minutes. I then left him alone and came back after about ten minutes, only to be absolutely stunned by his work.

The first thing that struck me was the amazing amount of detail he had put into each drawing, which was done in only ten minutes! Curiously, as you can see, he wrote *Stars' War*, which, although represents a misspelling of the original title, one could make the argument that it actually makes more sense, at least to the uninitiated *Star Wars* fan: shouldn't there be just *one* war that takes place amongst *many* stars instead of many wars occurring on only one? I'm sure that his spelling choice wasn't the result of a ten-minute philosophical analysis but rather the result of translating 'Guerra de las Galaxias', which in Spanish means War of the Galaxies, directly to English.

But perhaps, the most valuable message in these drawings is its underlying violent nature. OFC damage, especially secondary to traumatic injuries, can lead to aggressive behaviour, anxiety and depression. No doubt that the fighter jet and the Tiger Tank depicted his underlying emotional state. After looking at these images, Vanessa was unpleasantly surprised; she felt perturbed both at the violent nature of the images and at the impressive detail that he wasn't apparently able to achieve before (at least in such a short amount of time!). Something had obviously changed in Renato's brain, and it wasn't good.

With the available clinical and radiological information, we knew quite a bit by now. Essentially, Renato had suffered a seizure due to a slow growing tumour in his frontal lobe, which had also been leading to noticeable changes in his behaviour and personality for the past two months. However, we still didn't know if the tumour was cancer or something else.

Answering this question, by far, would be the most challenging aspect of Renato's case. First of all, an MRI would have been ideal in order to further define the lesion; however, there was no chance of obtaining one in less than 3–4 weeks; it was very costly, and it had to be approved by a long list of people. And also, it wasn't uncommon for ongoing licitation disputes between rivalling companies over the legal rights to sell the MRI services to the Almenara Hospital, to paralyse the service indefinitely. So, an MRI was out of the question. We needed a quick solution, something that could quickly guide our therapeutic efforts. On the other hand, a brain biopsy was another potential avenue, but the neurosurgeons were reluctant to do so, mainly because of the location of the tumour. They felt that the procedure could cause further damage. So, that alternative was out of the equation as well.

These sorts of impasses were a daily problem, the type that every doctor in Peru could attest to. When faced with a bureaucratic brick wall, as we all knew very well, creative ("out-of-the-box") thinking – the artistic flipside of science – was required. A bit of tangential thinking can go a long way in medicine. That ingenuity wasn't guesswork; it was based on epidemiological knowledge. Every country has a different set of medical conditions that are more common to its demographics. In Peru, for example, a developing country with high indices of poverty and very poor sanitary conditions, infectious diseases are very prevalent. Infections such as toxoplasmosis, cysticercosis, cryptococcosis, HIV/AIDS, tuberculosis (TB), trypanosomiasis (Chagas disease), dengue, brucellosis, herpes virus, cytomegalovirus, aspergillosis, paracoccidiomycosis and candida were almost always high on the list of differential diagnoses. Amongst these, tuberculosis is, by far, the most common infection. According to the World Health Organisation, in 2017, there were roughly 37,000 estimated cases of TB in Peru, second only to Brazil, with 91,000. In the whole of South America, the overall risk of TB is 46.2 cases per 100,000, as opposed to in North America, in which the prevalence was about 3.3 cases per 100,000 people. Furthermore, Peru has the highest burden of multidrug resistant (MDR)-TB in South America. In the United States, Spain and the UK – countries with less poverty and much better sanitary conditions – these infections are extremely rare.

On the other hand, cancers, including brain tumours, are much more prevalent in developed countries, as opposed to poorer ones. Therefore, purely based on the local epidemiology, the tumour growing in Renato's brain was most likely, *not* cancer. However, at this stage, we could neither prove nor disprove this.

Time was not on our side. Whatever was in Renato's brain, it was *growing*. His personality was growing intolerable; he suffered several more seizures and seemed to be losing the will to fight. In order to buy some time, I did a lumbar puncture, which unfortunately, only provided information we already knew; there was an active source of inflammation in the central nervous system (CNS), but no further clues. His chest X-ray was normal, but his TB skin test was positive, indicating that he had been infected with TB at some point in his life (latent TB). Could it have reactivated for some reason?

We had to do something. After discussing his case in our weekly team meeting, we reached the conclusion that, based on the information available to us, Renato most likely had a 'tuberculoma', which the rarest form of CNS tuberculosis, account for only 1% of all cases. In fact, about 30% of this 1% manifest has multiple, small growths in the brain; Renato had only one growth. Following this, we started him on antituberculosis treatment, which consisted of four drugs: Isoniazid, Rifampin, Pyrazinamide and Ethambutol. The rationale behind this approach was straightforward: if his symptoms and the size of the growth improved over a short period of time, then our assumption was correct. If it didn't, then we were all in deep trouble.

Well, we were lucky. After about three weeks, he started to improve! Not only did his behaviour improve but the swelling also started to improve. And after about six weeks, the tumour size also started to shrink.

Hence, the tumour 'had' to be tuberculosis and not cancer. That was the good news. However, the bad news was that something else, which had been flying below our radars, had been chipping away at Renato's immune system, allowing the previously latent TB to gradually emerge. This wouldn't be easy to find. The majority of such diseases and infections had already been excluded, including HIV and certain cancers, such as lung, pancreas, prostate and colon.

We had to dig deeper, to think harder. So, for the next week, we investigated everything from autoimmune diseases to metabolic disorders. It was bittersweet to keep getting normal results, to keep discovering that all our ideas were incorrect.

As I was reaching my wit's end, I decided to imagine that Renato was a woman and go through the differential diagnoses I would have proposed in this case. Could there be something I wasn't thinking of simply because Renato was a man and not a woman? Was there something that, as a man, made him more prone to have? This was a technique – more like a trick, to be honest – that I had discovered early on in my career. It made me think outside the box, to unblock my cognitive stalemate. As soon as I started thinking of breast, uterus and ovarian cancers, their male counterparts – testicles and male breasts – immediately popped to mind. Could Renato have a testicular or breast cancer?

As soon as I arrived next morning, the first thing I did was to examine Renato again, from head to toe. Once again, I didn't find anything out of the ordinary, in particular, no testicular nor breast tumour. Nevertheless, I requested alpha-feto-protein (AFP), human chorionic gonadotropin (HCG) and lactate dehydrogenase (LDH) levels in blood, which are testicular tumour markers. Four days later, we had our results: very high levels of HCG and LDH without any raise in AFP. That same day, he had an ultrasound that confirmed a small tumour with moderate swelling. Renato had a testicular cancer called 'seminoma'! We finally had our answer! Case closed!

Bizarrely, having brain tuberculosis was the best thing that could have happened to him! If he had never suffered the seizure, he would have never known about his testicular cancer. I'm sure that he would have found out sooner or later about it, but as with every cancer, the sooner you treat it, the better it is. If he had not had a seizure, who knows when he would have discovered that he had a seminoma? Quite simply: the tuberculoma saved his life.

After about four months, I saw Vanessa and Renato in my clinic for his first follow up appointment after being discharged. By that time, he had already undergone successful testicular surgery; he had continued to take his anti-tuberculosis treatment without any complications and his brain MRI showed an almost complete resolution of the frontal lobe tuberculoma. And more importantly, his behaviour had returned to normal.

Before the appointment was over, I told him if he wanted back the drawings of the tank and fighter jet, perhaps as memorabilia of those dangerous and odd days. To this, he replied, "No, thanks. I've tried to make those drawings after going home, and I've never been able to do them again. I would hate to feel depressed about not being able to do things that only a tumour enabled me to do."

For me, however, these drawings represented a life-long neurological lesson: *not all brain damage implies a loss of function.* Injury to certain parts of the brain can paradoxically create *new capacities*, which some patients feel nostalgic about losing. Renato didn't want his drawings back because he longed for the days when his damaged brain could bedazzle him and lead him to think of the most awe-inspiring ideas. Who was I to debate with him over this? I too have always struggled with my own unpredictable and many times uncontrollable fugue of thoughts. If I could get rid of them, I probably wouldn't want to do so either.

Alberto

In Peru, there is no such thing as social 'unemployment help'. There's no such thing as 'Well-Fare', like in the United States or a furlough scheme as we've seen come into effect in the UK following the coronavirus pandemic or as the financial help that I obtained in Spain when I lost my job (in 2012). In Peru, if you are sacked from your job, you will receive a lump sum settlement from your employer (in some cases) based on the amount of time you've worked for them, but you will not be supported by any sort of government or social scheme. In fact, this was one of the major problems in Peru during coronavirus outbreak: millions of workers were suddenly facing unemployment with nothing to fall back on, without any sort of government help at all. They're subsistence and livelihood was fully dependent on their employers' good will. The vast majority of workers in Peru make barely enough money to make ends meet, without any capacity whatsoever to create savings. So, when they lose their jobs, they are usually left dangling in the wind.

If you are self-employed, the situation is even worse. Taxi drivers in Lima, especially up until about ten years ago, were mainly self-employed. Essentially, to be a 'taxi driver' in Peru, the only thing you had to do was to stick a label that said 'TAXI' on the front window of your car. That was it.

Obviously, this led to an immense number of kidnappings, rapes, robberies, etc. By no means am I saying that all taxi drivers were untrustworthy or dangerous, but you really never knew for sure if the car you were getting into was being driven by a nice person or a psychopath.

Eventually, taxi services in Peru became more formalised. Taxi companies started to develop, hiring drivers with background medical and mental health checks, as also, criminal records. However, because company-taxi drivers had to hand in a percentage of their income to the owners of these companies, many drivers preferred to fly solo. Obviously, those that remained self-employed ran the risk of not finding too many customers, but on the other hand, their earnings would entirely stay with them.

Well, Alberto was a 61-year-old self-employed taxi driver, who lived with his wife, widowed son and three grandchildren in a very small house in Magdalena (one of the inner districts of Lima). Before becoming a taxi driver, he was a carpenter, making very elaborate wooden furniture, which he sold on the weekends.

I didn't learn these things from Alberto but from his wife Beatriz. I met them both one night in the AE after they arrived in the hospital ambulance. As I was waiting for Alberto to come out of the CT machine, Beatriz filled me in on his family background. She also told me that he was a smoker, had hypertension, diabetes and high cholesterol levels: the perfect recipe for a stroke.

As they were both sitting at home watching TV, Alberto suddenly felt a tingling feeling run down his right upper and lower limb. "I didn't know what was going on with him. He suddenly stopped speaking and looked petrified," said

Beatriz. Soon after, he had a massive seizure and, in the process, became incontinent and bit his tongue. By the time he arrived to the hospital, he had partially recovered but was profoundly weak and disorientated.

As he was rolled out of the CT machine, I noticed that his face was asymmetric and that he was drooling profusely. His blood pressure was extremely high, at 210/120 mmHg. The CT image was unquestionable: Alberto had suffered a large intracerebral bleed, most likely as a consequence of high blood pressure.

That night, he suffered three more seizures. He had vomited in the process and aspirated into his lungs. His blood pressure remained very high and his temperature started to creep up.

After a gruelling night of intense treatment and monitoring, Alberto was able to gain some degree of stability by 8 am the next morning. By midday, although his blood pressure was still high, it wasn't as critical as when he arrived. Furthermore, following the administration of anti-seizure medications, he didn't suffer further seizure episodes.

By midday, he was already on the neurology ward. I remember sitting down next to him, trying to obtain a bit more of information, but unfortunately, after I asked him a couple of questions, the only response I got from him was 'difficult, difficult, difficult'. He kept repeating these words over and over. I asked him if he could understand me and his response was 'difficult, difficult'. He was unable to speak or comprehend; the medical terminology is expressive and receptive aphasia (global aphasia) and this was directly related to the fact that the intracerebral bleed had occurred on the left frontal and temporal lobes of his brain, i.e., in the 'language centres'. More so, he was also profoundly weakened down the right side of his body.

In a heartbeat, Alberto's life had changed forever. One minute he was watching television at home with his wife and family, the next, he was unable to speak, comprehend or move the upper and lower limbs on the right side. Just like that. His taxi-driving days were done for good…Or so I thought!

Little did I know that Alberto had the heart of a lion. Essentially, after two months of admission, intense physiotherapy and medical management, he had recovered the mobility in his right arm and the capacity to comprehend verbal speech. Unfortunately, though, his right leg was still very weak, and he wasn't able to properly speak, even though he could signal with his left hand and nod. He had made an impressive recovery. I think that the pictures of his grandchildren and of Beatriz lined up next to his bed was his main inspiration and driving force to keep going.

About two weeks later, he was successfully discharged and scheduled to be seen in clinic after three months. The day he went home, I asked him what he was going to do about work. Driving a taxi was – at least in my mind – out of the question. However, instead of acknowledging his limitation, he winked at me and gave me a half grin, as if to say 'you'll see'.

Two months later, I saw him in clinic. He hobbled into clinic using crutches and wearing a big smile on his face. His speech has slightly improved, but his leg strength was still very poor.

He had managed to conjure up the most ingenious solution to not being able to drive. He sawed a broomstick in half and tied one of halves to his right leg, so that the stick surpassed his foot (In Peru, the steering wheel is on the left). By doing this, the stick would act like his foot; he would push the stick with his right hand or retrieve it, when he wanted to accelerate or to reduce speed, respectively. When he wanted to use the brake, he would use his left foot, which was absolutely fine. In order for this daring plan to work, he had to change his mechanical car for an automatic one, which he was fortunately able to do through a generous friend who owned a car dealership.

As for his speech, he had a solution to that too. He prepared a series of different cards with prepared answers, such as 'you're welcome', 'ten soles', 'too far', and 'I can take you'. Occasionally, he would be able to half-way pronounce a couple of words, which would cause him great joy, but in general, he relied on his cards.

I was so impressed that I asked him to drive me home just to witness his outstanding feet of courage, ingenuity and determination. As we were riding home, I felt embarrassed with myself for having ever complained about the meaningless 'problems' in my life. This man was singlehandedly proving how human resourcefulness can overcome almost any obstacle and how, if there's a will, there's most certainly, a way.

Peru is full of people like Alberto. People who have used their creativity and ingenuity to overcome an illness. People who are willing to do 'anything' in order to keep living and functioning in society, people who are true survivors. As you walk down the streets of Lima, you come across many homeless men, women and children, many of which have suffered either physical or mental illness, who try their very best to survive under the most strenuous conditions. Alberto and I knew that his haemorrhagic stroke could have permanently disabled him had he not pushed forward with such determination. We also knew – although no one said it – that had he been permanently disabled, he would have probably ended up on the streets.

Sometimes in life, we all need to be put to the test, to be removed from our comfort zones and to be left to our own devices to see how we respond. And I don't just mean physically; I mean intellectually as well. If we only do and think what makes us feel comfortable and safe, first of all, we will never change, and second of all, we'll never know how much we can accomplish. It's not a matter of waiting to be in Alberto's position in order to become creative but rather, to do this 'now'. Imagine how much you could actually achieve if you thought and acted like Alberto did, but as you are right now, *in* health! And on the other hand, if you are not in the best of health, think of how much you can still achieve through will power and determination.

Daniel

He seemed to be in peace, yet he was completely helpless. The rays of sunshine coming through the back blinds must have appeased him, if it was only to give him a bit of temporary warmth and to keep him in touch with the outside world, which, very sadly, was inaccessible to him. His flaccid limbs gave the impression of a pre-emptive surrender whilst the multiple monitors and the numerous intravenous lines betrayed his poor prognosis. What could have possibly gone wrong with Daniel, the 17-year-old boy who laid before me that summer morning?

During sunrise, hospital wards are usually quiet enough to observe and to hear the clinical subtleties that go unnoticed during the rest of the day, such as breathing patterns, involuntary movements, antalgic positions, conscious awakening, orientation in space and in some cases, if you're sufficiently observant, sunlight-induced photophobia.

For about ten minutes, as the sun was giving birth to a new day, I had unfettered access to each of Daniel's unconscious actions: from his shallow breathing to his rhythmic thoracic movements and from his occasional limb twitching to the rapid eye movements below his closed eyelids. The large nasogastric tube revealed that he had difficulty swallowing and the nasal supply of oxygen implied a difficulty, albeit mild, to breath. His overgrown toenails implied that he had been bedbound for a long time and the wrinkles on his skin, so well illuminated by the sunrays behind him, represented widespread muscle atrophy. Next to his bed, hung a urinary catheter, which represented yet another faulty system.

The image of such a frail young man was deeply troubling to me. If I, as a young doctor, had the unique opportunity to enter Daniel's life at his most vulnerable time, then I also had the moral obligation to do as much as I could for him, for as long as I was given the privilege to do so. Early on in my career, I learned that being a doctor doesn't just give you the right to witness and to listen to someone's problems but more importantly, it enables you to *do something* about them; in medicine, *knowledge without action is useless and action without knowledge is dangerous.*

So, having acquired a large amount of information during those precious ten sunlit minutes, I now had to do something with it. As I scrolled through his notes, Teresa, the nurse in charge summarised his recent history: "He was transferred over from a hospital in Cuzco only two days ago whilst you were on call. Apparently, he was there for almost four weeks before coming here. No one knows what's wrong with him. They think he might have had some sort of viral encephalitis, but who knows?"

As I passed the pages of his encyclopaedia-sized clinical history, he started to wake up, as if he knew we were talking about him. "Daniel, can you hear me?" I asked. "Can you see me?" He slowly nodded to both questions. "Can you tell me the names of your parents?" He gazed over to me, locking his dilated pupils onto mine – as if to prove that he 'absolutely' understood the question and that I shouldn't prematurely give up on his cognitive abilities despite his general appearance – and very slowly, murmured a couple of unintelligible syllables whilst a few tears ran down his face. He 'knew' the answer; he just couldn't say it.

Just imagine for one moment that you were Daniel: an adolescent boy, lying in a hospital bed for the past month, in a different city 400 miles from home, unable to move nor to swallow and that you can't even state the names of your parents when asked. Dreadful, right? For me, it was disheartening. However, at that moment, if I would have allowed my natural, empathetic response to displace my rational thought process, then undoubtedly, my medical judgement would have been immediately clouded and all those refined clinical observations made under the quietness of the morning sunlight would have been lost to emotions. In medicine, one must learn to gracefully acknowledge unfortunate situations but at the same time, have the ability to swiftly focus on how to remedy them, for if you ruminate in your emotions for too long, the solution to the clinical problem can very easily drift away.

After a couple of minutes, enough for both of us to absorb the impact of his inability to speak, I moved on to the rest of his examination. Beyond scarcely wiggling his fingers and his toes, his toneless limbs laid lifelessly at the bedside. His expressionless face revealed the involvement of his facial muscles as well. Even the muscles responsible for moving his eyes were compromised, as evidenced by his near inability to bring on saccadic movements. Hidden muscles, also, such as the ones responsible for his swallowing, were also involved. Making use of the nasogastric tube inevitable.

On the other hand, he was perfectly able to distinguish all forms of sensory stimuli, from pinprick pain to blunt touch and from vibratory perception to distinguishing between hot and cold. From a cognitive perspective, he was fully capable of comprehension, but as already noted, he was unable to verbalise his answers. Without a doubt, this particular limitation represented the highest psychological burden for Daniel. He was in a dire state.

Later on, that day, I met his mum Rosa and his 19-year-old sister, Margarita. As I told them, "I only have a single image of Daniel. I need a movie of him, so to speak. Let's go back to when it all started. Don't leave anything out, even if you think it's not important."

Margarita spoke first. "He was fine until about four months ago, when he started to have seizures. We took him to a doctor who told us it 'was nothing' and that it would 'go away'."

Rosa then continued by saying, "We also noticed that his behaviour was changing, that he became gradually quieter and more withdrawn." They also told me that approximately three months before his admission to the hospital in Cuzco, he started to suffer recurrent falls. His strength started to fade away, eventually leading him to become bedridden. Almost at the same time, not only did his swallowing capacities start to fail but also his capacity to speak slowly faded away. Eventually, he completely stopped talking and moving. The only movement came when he had a seizure, which sadly was four or five times a day.

Rosa assured me that Daniel had been fit and well up until this terrible situation started. He didn't have any addictions, never took drugs or drank alcohol. And in fact, he was a pretty good athlete in school. From family perspective, his dad had died when he was only three years old in a car accident and Rosa was mildly hypertensive and diabetic. Margarita had no previous medical issues at all.

I remember being so enthralled by the case that I took his notes home with me that night, something that could have landed me in a lot of trouble. But I didn't care, because it was the only way of reviewing such a huge amount of information without distractions. Going through all this valuable information would have been impossible during normal working hours.

The first thing that stuck out whilst reviewing the notes was the numerous – practically daily – amount of seizures Daniel suffered, despite being treated with three antiepileptic drugs. The term 'myoclonic episodes', which are a particular type of seizure that present as short-lived, 'shock-like' jerks of the limbs, was written on almost every page since the day of his admission. Occasionally, however, he would also have 'grand-mal seizures', i.e., generalised seizures, that lead to loss of consciousness, tongue-biting and urinary incontinence.

On the other hand, there were multiple entries from the various therapist teams, detailing the difficulties they encountered during each session: his speech, his swallowing and his overall mobility were progressively worsening despite their best efforts.

Another section of the notes recorded all the investigations that had been carried out during his hospitalisation, which included a brain MRI, a spinal cord MRI, two lumbar punctures and a series of blood cultures and tests assessing for possible kidney, liver, coagulation and electrolytes abnormalities, all of which were normal. All these results, taken together, had excluded most of the 'usual suspects': meningitis, encephalitis, liver and kidney failure (which can sometimes cause neurological complications), electrolyte disturbances, multiple sclerosis, stroke, tumours, and HIV together with all the opportunistic infections that can arise because of it, such as tuberculosis, amongst others. He also was tested for illicit drug toxicity and that too was negative.

However, even though the vast majority of results were normal, there were two very subtle abnormalities that had enormous value. First of all, a muscle enzyme called Creatine Kinase (CK) was moderately high, and this indicated that his muscles were undergoing damage. Secondly, another enzyme, Lactate Dehydrogenase (LDH), was also high in his bloodstream, which not only reemphasised that his muscles were suffering but also that his internal metabolism had shifted from aerobic (oxygen-based) to 'anaerobic' (glucose-based), which occurs when oxygen transport to the tissues is compromised. It is considerably 'less efficient' in generating energy (Adenosine Triphosphate or simply, ATP) than its aerobic counterpart.

After about five days of admission, the CK and LDH levels had doubled. Not coincidentally, due to the increased excretion of the degraded muscle products in urine, the kidneys started to fail. It's important to mention that CK and LDH are not specific markers for any specific disease; they can be elevated in numerous conditions, each of which, one way or another, end up causing muscle degradation. On the other hand, a new lumbar puncture revealed that there were elevated levels of LDH in the cerebrospinal fluid as well.

Given these results, an electromyography (EMG) – which is a test to assess the integrity of the muscular system – should have been done; however, it wasn't, because this technology wasn't available in Cuzco at the time. Unfortunately, we weren't doing much better in Lima either, because our EMG machine was broken.

So, after about one week of admission, I was certain of what Daniel *did not* have, yet I was still no closer to having a definitive diagnosis. The multisystem involvement indicated that his problem was generalise rather than local, more likely caused by an underlying metabolic disorder. However, these tend to have a genetic aetiology and, as such, are usually inherited. Daniel's young age and his elevated CK and LDH levels pointed towards an inherited muscle disorder; however, there was nothing in his family history to suggest such a disease. Therefore, this was one more set of conditions that I had to remove from my rapidly shrinking list of differential diagnoses.

As I ran through all the results, I couldn't conceive how Daniel had become so unwell in such a short period of time, without any major finding to show for it. But then, by pure chance, I struck gold. I would think of something that, in the most unexpected and unintended way, led to a diagnosis!

What if it's some sort of heavy metal intoxication? I wondered. It certainly seemed like a viable option, at least at this late stage of the game. So, I set out to request every heavy metal I could think of and after a couple of weeks, low and behold, Daniel had a very high level of copper in his urine, yet interestingly, a very low level in his bloodstream.

Nearly every doctor, young and old, associates the word copper with Wilson disease. It's like a knee-jerk reaction.

However, after my own knee-jerk conclusion, I realised that it couldn't be. Why? Well, because this condition causes involuntary movements, liver dysfunction and typical brain MRI findings, none of which Daniel had. However, just to be sure, I requested ceruloplasmin levels – the main copper-binding protein in the body, which is typically low in Wilson's disease – and it was normal. Finally, just to put the final nail in the Wilson coffin, I asked for an ophthalmologist to exclude the presence of the characteristic Keiser-Fleisher (KF) rings – a pathognomonic eye sign of Wilson's disease, which manifests as dark rings encircling the iris – and they were nowhere to be found. However, quite amazingly, while he was assessing Daniel's eyes, he unveiled an unexpected piece of the puzzle: bilateral cataracts! For the doctors reading this book, I'm sure that with this new information, you can think of several new diagnoses!

So, let's see: we have a 17-year-old boy who has elevated CK and LDH levels, daily seizures, cognitive regression, pronounced muscle wasting, bilateral cataracts and elevated copper in urine yet low copper in blood!

To my inexperienced young eyes, Daniel's copper results obeyed an underlying metabolic disorder. The crucial question for me was: is there a link between his progressive muscle atrophy and the copper results? More so, where did the cataracts fit into all of this?

These results led me to several nights of research-induced insomnia! My reasoning was as follows: if a persistently elevated level of LDH implies a problem with Daniel's 'aerobic metabolism', then, almost invariably, it pointed me towards a problem originating in the mitochondria, which is a vital substructure of the cell, in charge of generating the body's energy (ATP), amongst many other functions. Mitochondrial disorders tend to be inherited. So, although there was no family history to support such a problem, I decided to keep investigating for this mitochondrial-based disorder.

Day after day, it was the only thing I could think about. Very frustratingly, every time an explanation seemed to appear in the distance, an unexpected piece of new information, which usually appeared from a minuscule footnote in a crumbling book from the hospital's library, would immediately disprove it.

However, one Saturday evening, as I was immersed in the depths of the 'electron transport chain' (ETC) – a vital biochemical cascade that takes place within the mitochondria – I was suddenly paralysed with elation: I read that copper actually participates in the ETC process! Could this mean that the low copper represented a flaw in the mitochondrial machinery? Was this the link I was desperately looking for? Furthermore, if this was the case, then it would almost guarantee that Daniel had a mitochondrial disorder! I couldn't breathe. Literally. I remember jumping up and down like a child with a new toy. It was one of the most exhilarating moments of my life. Maybe I was wrong, but the fact that my stubborn intuition, against all odds, had led me to presumably unite two distinct and apparently unrelated ends of Daniel's clinical spectrum and, accomplishing it with deductive reasoning, was enough to make me emotionally fly. To this day, 13 years later, every time I either read or diagnose a patient with a mitochondrial disease, I remember this feeling.

The purity of such a beautiful emotion can never be predetermined nor anticipated; it must emerge from the naturalness of a genuine epiphany, which sweeps you off your feet and leaves you blissfully exhausted and thirsty for more. It leaves a permanent mark on your soul.

Those painstaking weeks of sleepless nights were suddenly validated by the reassurance that the human body's exquisitely complex inner workings follow a logic that is accessible to those who study it with passion and patience. It felt as if I had earned the right to understand Daniel's condition.

After about 20 to 30 minutes, the time it took me to calm down and regain focus, I sat down again to carry on reading, to see where copper would lead me. Not long after, I read that within the same ETC pathway, deficiencies in antioxidants such as 'Coenzyme Q' can lead to mitochondrial dysfunction as well. Copper and coenzyme Q, within the ETC, are closely linked in function.

All this newly discovered information was exhilarating, to say the least. What if Daniel's levels of coenzyme Q were also deficient? Obviously, we hadn't tested for this in blood, so there was no other way of proving this with certainty. However, up until this point, my intuitions had guided me well, through a confusing and counterintuitive maze.

That evening, as I rode the wave of exhilaration, I ran to the nearest pharmacy and naively asked if they sold coenzyme Q! To my surprise, not only did they have it but it came in all sorts of presentations, from creams and lotions, to capsules and tables. Never in my wildest dreams did I think that a substance with such a scientific profundity, hidden away in the depths of the mitochondria, could have been converted into such a wide variety of commercially available 'health enhancers' and 'rejuvenators'. Keeping in mind that I couldn't obviously bathe Daniel in coenzyme Q lotion three times a day, I decided to buy a bottle of 100 capsules that I still remember paying for with a pocket full of coins, which clicked and clanked all the way to the pharmacy.

For the next ten days, three times a day, I would dissolve the coenzyme Q capsule in a bit of water (not too scientific I have to admit!) and administer it through his nasogastric tube. Amazingly, after five or six days of this, not only did his limbs started to get stronger but also his eyes started to move better. For me, as a naïve and inexperienced second-year, 25-year-old neurology trainee, this response was larger than life.

Rosa and Margarita were utterly surprised to see his improvement, even if it was very small. Put yourself in Rosa and Margarita's shoes for a minute: imagine that your son or brother, who has barely moved, spoken or looked at you for weeks, and that suddenly, he's able to freely and voluntarily shift his gaze towards you, make slightly clearer sounds – that now have become somewhat intelligible – and that he now has the ability to squeeze your hand and even to offer you a wonderful grin! This was the stuff of dreams. I remember telling myself whilst I witnessed Rosa, Margarita and Daniel reunite in flesh and spirit, *this is what makes all the sleepless nights, all the non-stop studying and all the hours away from home completely worth it.*

As I write this chapter, with the benefit of 13 years of nostalgic hindsight, in all honesty, I still don't know if the low levels of copper in blood were 'directly' linked to Daniel's disease, nor can I say with 'absolute certainty' that he had a deficiency in coenzyme Q. Essentially, the latter was presumed to be the case, solely based on the former. However, for the sceptics – including myself – quite frankly, the constellation of his young age, progressive muscle wasting, bilateral cataracts, refractory seizures and elevated LDH and CK was already enough to make a very strong case in favour of a mitochondrial disease. However, because there was no family history – the most important of all risk factors – it seemed unreasonable to suggest it. For me to have assumed that the abnormal copper levels were simply a 'coincidence' or perhaps, something completely unrelated to the combined clinical and laboratory results seemed more unreasonable! Finally, as soon as I learned that copper and coenzyme Q work in close connection within the ETC in the mitochondria, it sealed the deal for me, and from that point on, I was absolutely convinced that Daniel *had* to have a mitochondrial disease.

Now came the hard part. How could I reconcile all of this with the fact that there was no family history supportive of a mitochondrial disorder? How was I to square this circle? There could only be one answer: 'Daniel had to be adopted.'

It took me a couple of days to build up the courage to ask Rosa if she was Daniel's biological mum. Once the loaded question landed, the expression of absolute disbelief on Rosa's face was painful to witness. It was so bad that I wished I had never asked. "How do you know? I've never told anyone, including Margarita," Rosa said.

"Well, after seeing Daniel's response to the coenzyme Q, it seemed like the only reasonable explanation," I explained.

As I told Rosa, 'each and every' one of our mitochondria are inherited from our mothers. *None of them* come from our fathers. Hence, any mitochondrial disease has maternal inheritance. More so, as seen in the graphic below, in each cell of our bodies, there is nuclear DNA (N) and mitochondrial (M) DNA. As the arrow indicates, the mitochondrial DNA is inherited purely through the material line.

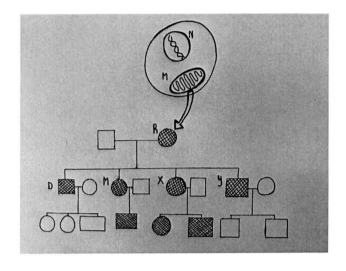

Let's imagine that Rosa (R), had a mitochondrial disorder and that, as seen in the pedigree, was not only the biological mother of Daniel (D) and Margarita (M) but also of another daughter (X) and of another son (Y). In this case, she would have passed along her mitochondria to *all* her offspring: D, M, X and Y. If either Daniel or Y had children, none of them would have a mitochondrial disease, because their children would have inherited all of their mitochondria from the mothers. Instead, if either Margarita or X had children, invariably, they would inherit their mother's pathological mitochondria.

Now, despite all the work done and despite all the knowledge we acquired over these weeks, without a muscle biopsy, the job wasn't done. A muscle biopsy is the gold standard for the diagnosis of mitochondrial pathologies.

Obtaining a muscle biopsy was the last hurtle to overcome. And might I add, it wasn't a small one.

Once again, frustratingly, we arrive to same unforgiving Peruvian problem in social medicine: lack of resources. As the reader no doubt already predicts, there wasn't a muscle biopsy service in the hospital. Just like in the case of Adriana's vital blood investigations, the only way of obtaining it was to outsource it to a private provider, and this was a very expensive undertaking. So, as the reader most likely already foresees, all the junior doctors quickly rallied around Daniel, each one pitching in whatever he or she could afford. Rosa and Margarita also gave some money but very little, as they were very poor and had been sleeping in the hospital because they couldn't afford anything else. After five days, we're able to obtain the necessary amount of money to pay for the biopsy. It had been a Herculean task, because the price of biopsy was almost 2000 dollars (about 1700 sterling)! Nevertheless, we did it! And might I add, the hospital did not supply coenzyme Q either, so we also had to pay for this.

After about 15 days, we had our pathological diagnosis, i.e., the final diagnosis. Daniel had 'Myoclonic Epilepsy with Red Ragged Fibres' (MERRF). It was an outstanding diagnosis, one which finally proved that Daniel's problems were due to an inherited mitochondrial problem. Very sadly, there is no specific treatment for MERRF. Essentially, it doesn't have a cure; it can only be managed symptomatically. After researching this diagnosis, I was pleased – and relieved, to be perfectly honest – that MERRF is normally managed with coenzyme Q, B complex vitamins and levocarnitine (L-carnitine).

Before I mentioned the diagnosis to Daniel, Rosa made me promise not to tell him that he was adopted, nor to tell Margarita. Neither of them knew. Of course, it wasn't my place to mention anything, so I was happy to guarantee that Daniel would never find out from me. On the other hand, after the four of us discussed the implications of such a difficult diagnosis, the only thing they all wanted was to go back to Cuzco. They all knew that there wasn't much more time for Daniel on this Earth, so they wanted to spend whatever time he had left in the land he called home. And so, after about four days, they all returned to Cuzco but not before thanking me and all of the neurology team for all our efforts. Rosa actually gave me a small handwritten letter that said (translated from Spanish), "Thank you, Doctor Canepa, for your kindness and patience. Daniel cannot speak, but I know he's also grateful. Hopefully, there will be a cure for this horrible disease one day."

I never saw any of them again. Sadly, I later found out that Daniel had died only three months after leaving the hospital, peacefully in his home, next to Rosa and Margarita.

My initial reaction to his death was sadness, rapidly followed by frustration and anger. Since my internship, I had witnessed first-hand, almost on a daily basis, the numerous deficiencies of the Peruvian health system and how it had a direct impact on patient care. I learned that many diagnostic tests and procedures that are widely available in the US and in Europe were considered to be a luxury in developing countries, such as Peru. I remember the bittersweet taste after reading English-written neurology journals and books during these early years of my career; it always felt like I was gaining a wealth of inapplicable knowledge! And yet, although it was very frustrating, it was also giving me an opportunity to prove that *a lack of resources does not necessarily entail a 'lack of resourcefulness'!*

Thinking, the source of all resourcefulness, is one of the main hallmarks of our species. Not only is it one of the most precious tools of our existence but also, it's free of charge, available at all times and to all people and can be used in all circumstances of life, regardless of poverty and hardships. The only cost incurred by thinking is the effort you put into it. Daniel taught me that implementing that resourcefulness leads to acquiring new information in the process. He taught me that if I had done a muscle biopsy on the first day of his arrival, I wouldn't have learned everything I did in the process. He taught me that the beauty behind remarkable cases doesn't reside in directly leaping to the conclusion with a biopsy, for example, but rather, that it's found in the painstaking process of putting the clinical pieces together with intellectual grit and passion. Learning about Daniel's diagnosis taught me about my own character and that, perhaps, was Daniel's greatest lesson.

On the most basic level, the doctor-patient relationship essentially represents the act of 'one human being taking care of another'. It is a co-dependent act of medical altruism and patient trust. Neither altruism nor trust should be conditioned by the potential outcome. Therefore, as a doctor, a terminally ill patient should neither condition your altruism nor hinder your efforts, because if there's one thing I've learned throughout the years – especially as a neurologist – is that, although you might not be able to cure a patient, you can always endeavour to alleviate their pain and improve their quality of life, no matter how little of it might be left. Giving coenzyme Q and obtaining a muscle biopsy was my way of not giving up on altruism, even though I knew how poor his chances of survival were.

On the other hand, as a patient, the trust you deposit in your doctor – if you wish to do so – should solely be based on his or her total commitment to your case. *For a doctor, trust is not a gift; it's a reward.* Despite all the difficulties, defeats and battles, Daniel and his family decided to reward me with their steadfast trust, and for that, I felt and still feel to this day, deeply honoured. I will always remember him.

Susy

Just as I was packing up my things to go home, out of the corner of my eye, I saw a new patient being rolled in from the far end of the ward. She was covered up to her eyes, which seemed to bulge out of her face, glancing in all directions, trying to make sense of the new environment.

It was already dark and the very long and narrow WWII-like wards with patients aligned side-to-side and the cold breeze entering through the open windows created an eerie ambiance, which couldn't have been anything but scary. Standing next to Susy was her 14-year-old son, Juan Carlos, holding her hand and behaving very bravely.

Soon after she settled in, I came over to introduce myself and to take an initial look at her medical history. She had been admitted form the AE, following a one-month history of progressive, generalised weakness, swallowing difficulties, blurred vision and crippling fatigue. About one week before coming in, she had lost the ability to walk for more than 10–20 yards, and practically all of her daily activities required some form of assistance. Her life had dramatically transformed; she couldn't work (selling vegetables in a food market close to the hospital), take her children to school or even use a fork and a knife without feeling fatigue. Her sister had recently arrived from Trujillo, a province 360 miles from

Lima, in order to help her with the children. Susy had escaped an abusive husband six months ago, so she was living on her own with three small children.

At 41 years of age, Susy had been generally fit and well without suffering from any previous medical condition. In fact, this was the first time she had ever been admitted to a hospital.

"Doctor, I've been feeling so tired. I don't know why. In the mornings, it's not that bad, but as the day goes by, the tiredness gets really bad, sometimes even with shortness of breath. And the worse thing is that my eyesight is also failing. I get a lot of double vision and my eyelids tend to close in the evenings."

As I listened to her, I was trying to think of all the diagnostic options, but as a last year medical student, my list wasn't too long! Nevertheless, I listened attentively, took notes and asked a lot of questions! All the while, Juan Carlos was next to her, responding to some of the questions his mum couldn't. He was a very responsible young man and clearly, a very caring son.

As she laid in bed, she wasn't able to raise her legs for more than 3–4 seconds. She could squeeze my hands without problems, but she couldn't raise her arms for more than a few seconds. In addition, all of the reflexes in upper and lower limbs were absent. Furthermore, when I asked her to move her eyes right to left, she couldn't move either one to the left and both eyes struggled to move upward as well (this was the reason for her double vision).

From a clinical point of view, she had myasthenia gravis, a neurological condition that causes muscle weakness that tends to worsen as the day goes by. Even the eye muscles can be affected, leading to double vision. In severe cases, it can cause weakness of respiratory muscles, which leads to respiratory failure. Susy was very unwell, practically on the verge of having respiratory failure. She had arrived at the hospital just in the nick of time.

After assessing her, I was desperate to find a neurologist who could help me diagnose this lady and put forth a plan for treating her; however, at such late hours, there was no neurologist to be found. So, I asked the ICU specialist to assess the patient. After he did so, he deemed her 'not for ICU' (yet) because her blood oxygen levels weren't 'too bad'. That meant that she would stay on the medical ward for the time being, very much like a ticking time bomb. I remember staying with her for another three hours, and when she finally fell asleep, I went home.

After a few more hours, I was back in the hospital. Fortunately, I was able to track down the neurologist, who was kind enough to leave his busy clinic to come and assess her. Indeed, she had myasthenia. She needed urgent treatment. Now, if Susy had been in Spain (perhaps) or in the UK (definitely), she would have gone to the ICU and received a treatment called intravenous immunoglobulin, which helps remove the dangerous antibodies circulating in her blood stream. However, not in Peru. First of all, immunoglobulin treatment is extremely expensive, and on the other hand, even if Susy had the money, it wouldn't have been available at such short notice. So, the only alternative was to give her oral treatment with a medication called pyridostigmine. Once the neurologist confirmed the diagnosis and requested the treatment, I was happy to call the pharmacy to push this forward ASAP. To my dismay, the pharmacy did not supply pyridostigmine!

As I put the phone down, the young Juan Carlos said, "I can run to the nearest pharmacy to see if they have it. But I don't know how much it will cost. I probably won't have enough."

To this, I replied, "Go ahead, don't worry about that. If they have it, we'll find some way to pay for it."

After about 30 minutes, Juan Carlos returned saying that the first pharmacy he asked did not stock it, but they gave him the address of another one to go to. The medication cost about 150 soles (roughly 35 dollars or 30 sterling). Neither Susy nor Juan Carlos had that amount of money on them, so all the trainees decided to chip in some money in order for Susy to get the medication she so desperately needed.

So, off he went. He clenched on to the money with one hand while he dried the sweat off his forehead with the other. He was on a mission to save his mum. Shortly after, he returned with a box of medications, profusely sweating and almost gasping for air. He had done it! We all had done it together!

It was unbelievable and tremendously rewarding and relieving to see how Susy started to improve after only four or five doses. After only a few days, she started to regain her strength, vision and general composition.

On the 4th day of her admission, whilst we were doing to the ward rounds one of the most intelligent doctors I've ever met – Dr Pinedo – who was a radiologist and an internist, decided to come along for the ward round as well. When such an eminence unexpectedly decides to attend a ward round, it's a very special opportunity to learn, but also it also creates a general sense of concern! Everyone was frightened they would be asked something they didn't know!

One of the doctors asked me to present Susy's case to Dr Pinedo. I remember standing next to her, surrounded by a semi-circle of doctors, medical students and nurses, all listening to my every word. And smack in the middle was Dr Pinedo!

Little by little, I went through the case – by memory, mind you (we were not allowed to read anything at all). Being the first case of myasthenia gravis I had ever encountered in my life, I was sure that Dr Pinedo would point out many things I didn't know, but I didn't mind. It felt oddly reassuring to have such an eminence take interest in such a complex case. I felt as if 'nothing could go wrong after this'.

Once I finished, he said, "Have you looked at her eyelids?"

I said, "Yes, sir, I have; they are no longer ptotic (fallen)."

To this, he responded, "No, I meant the lower eyelids. Are they pale inside?" Unfortunately, I hadn't. So, I immediately did so and saw that indeed, they were very pale (not the usual reddish colour she should have had). "She's probably anaemic because she's not been eating enough, probably because she is scared of choking." He then came close to her, looked at her fingers and said, "These fingers are as white as her lower eyelids. And their cold to touch. This is Raynaud phenomenon (which is a small vessel abnormality that affects fingers and toes)."

"Are you very thirsty throughout the day? Do you drink a lot of water?" he asked Susy directly.

"Yes, Doctor. I am constantly thirsty and have to go to the toilet frequently."

"Interesting," he said. "Is there anything else you would like to add?"

Susy replied, "Yes, I constantly have stomach-aches. It burns a lot, especially at night. And also, my stools are very dark, almost like tar."

"All of this is extremely interesting, Susy, because it seems like your myasthenia gravis, which is an autoimmune condition, is associated with other conditions that are also autoimmune: Raynaud's phenomenon, diabetes and even something called pernicious anaemia, which is usually associated by gastrointestinal problems. We also need to make sure you don't have a tumour (thymoma) in your chest, which could have generated the myasthenia gravis in the first place."

While Dr Pinedo was saying this, I could read Susy and Juan Carlos's mind. They were wondering how on earth would they afford to stay in the hospital that long and how were they going to pay for these tests. More so, if she did have a tumour, how was she going to pay for the surgery!

And as if by magic or telepathy, as soon as Dr Pinedo finished his explanation, he said, "...And don't worry about the costs of the tests. I'll make sure we make an arrangement with the hospital to help as much as possible." As soon as he said that, my level of admiration for this man elevated to levels I thought weren't possible: a brilliant doctor who had a heart of gold.

And so, during the following weeks, she underwent all the types of tests the hospital could offer, unveiling precisely what Dr Pinedo had suggested. She had diabetes, Raynaud's phenomena, a medium-sized thymoma and a very rare and interesting condition called: 'dysphagia lusoria' (Bayford-Autenrieth dysphagia), which causes difficulty swallowing due to an aberrant artery (the right subclavian artery); this can cause occasionally upper gastrointestinal bleeding and secondary anaemia. So, it seemed like the myasthenia gravis was a red herring for the choking episodes! It might have made them worse, but there was something already there before the myasthenia gravis started. It wasn't uncommon for Dr Pinedo to have types of 'oracle moments'.

Now we had Susy's case completely deciphered! And she was improving by the day. The only thing that was still pending was the thoracic surgery to remove the thymoma.

Despite Dr Pinedo's incredibly generous offering to cover the vast majority of the costs of the investigations, Susy still had to pay for the bed she was occupying. I don't remember the exact cost, but I think it was roughly 100 soles (about 25 dollars or 20 sterling) per day. And of course, there was still the matter of paying for the pyridostigmine!

Little did I know, but 14-year-old Juan Carlos had the solution! And it was absolutely beautiful. "I've been working," he said.

"What do you mean?" I responded.

"I was told that if I work doing gardening and other handy work around the hospital, I could pay for my mum's hospital bill this way."

I was flabbergasted by his mature decision and his show of courage, strength and humanism. Foreseeing the economic problem, he took it upon himself to speak to someone in the administration to find a solution. Simply remarkable. It just goes to show that where there's a will there's a way.

After almost four weeks of admission, Susy was ready to go home. And debt free! She came in very unwell and before going home had four new diagnoses, underwent a large thoracic surgery and her son had proven to be her knight in shining armour! Susy's care was an example of altruism, dedication, hard work and hope, on all levels: from Dr Pinedo's kind gesture to help with payments, to the junior doctors' money recollection for the pyridostigmine, to Juan Carlos's heroic efforts to work to pay off his mum's bills.

In the Loayza Hospital, what we didn't have in materials and medications, we had in altruism and dedication to our patients.

Almeria

One afternoon in June 2009, about one month after qualifying as a neurologist, whilst I was window-shopping outside a well-known bookstore in Lima, I suddenly received a phone call from my older brother, Dr Pablo Garibaldi, who said, "There's a job out here if you want it, but you need to answer me now."

"What do you mean? In Spain?" I asked.

"Yes, it's in Almeria. Do you want it?" Needless to say, my blissfully idle window-shopping evening came to an abrupt halt.

Although it sounded like a great opportunity, especially in my position as a young, recently qualified, inexperienced and unemployed neurologist, three problems immediately popped out; first, it was on the other side of the world, in a country in which I had never practised medicine before. Second, the job wasn't for a neurology post but for general medicine, mainly working in the emergency department and third, my fiancé Lorena, who led a very successful psychology practice in Lima, would not be able to go.

With all these obstacles, it would have been absurd of me to have entertained the idea for more than a few seconds. However, it took me just five minutes to say, "I'll see you soon, Pablo."

In order for the reader to understand my allegedly ludicrous decision, a brief description of the Peruvian employment and socio-economic reality at that time would certainly come in handy.

Historically, Lima has hosted one third of Peru's overall population, which represents roughly ten million people. This degree of overpopulation has consistently maintained the demand for jobs – in all fields – above and beyond the available supply. The centralisation of resources in Lima, from commerce to medical care, has consistently boosted rural migration, which in turn fuelled higher rates of unemployment and poverty. Essentially, apart from agriculture and mining, all other forms of industry are abundantly more available in the capital.

The Peruvian health care services have always been highly concentrated in Lima. In 2009, there was a total of 17,648 medical beds in Lima, which represented 39% of Peru's total hospital beds. Huancavelica, for example, the province where Adriana was born, had in 2009 only 382 beds for a population of 49, 570 people. In other words, only one bed per 129.7 people. Going back to Lima in 2009, considering a population of roughly 10 million, there was only one bed per 588 people!

On the other hand, as of 2018, there was a total of 82, 427 registered doctors in Peru, out of which, 45,235 worked in Lima. In other words, more than 50% of the medical workforce resided in Lima, i.e., in *one* of the other 25 regions. Huancavelica, for example, in 2018 had 291 doctors for a population of more than 50,000 people! No wonder Adriana's parents fled to Lima in 2003!

So, finding a job as a doctor in Lima, no matter what speciality, was extremely difficult. Very sadly, many of the doctors in Lima are forced to do other things that are not medicine in order to make a living, such as driving a taxi. Furthermore, even if you were lucky enough to have a job, the salary was very low, barely enough to cover basic needs. And depending on where you worked, your salary wasn't even guaranteed at the end of the month! During my first year of neurology training, I received my first salary eight months after starting! I remember making about 50 soles (12 sterling) for a 12-hour on call shift and 80 soles (20 sterling) for a 24-hour on call shift, which was always on a weekend.

As my training was coming to an end, my fear of unemployment was exponentially growing. I felt as if I wanted my training to continue just so I could have the guarantee of a job! In fact, that was a pretty common sentiment amongst specialist trainees. I had a friend who went into paediatric training after qualifying as a general surgeon. As he told one day, "At least I'll have a job for the next five years." After finishing his paediatric day job, he would perform bariatric surgeries from 5–7 pm in another hospital. Another friend of mine, who had trained in emergency medicine, worked in three different hospitals, just to make ends meet. He basically was never home. At some point, I too was considering applying to another speciality program, possibly in internal medicine.

Therefore, when Pablo suddenly told me 'there's a job for you', this had a powerful psychological effect on me; I felt a sense unburdening.

The offer came with the added bonus of a generous salary, which, of course, was appealing, especially because I was accustomed to earning the bear minimum, despite working seven days a week.

But the job wasn't for a neurologist! Why would I even consider it? Well, I figured that once I was in Spain, I could revalidate my neurology degree and eventually work as a neurologist. I had a licence to practise general medicine in Spain, so I would use that in the meantime. The important thing, in my mind, was to get a job 'in medicine'!

Finally, I had to convince Lorena! As the wonderful woman she has always been, I wasn't so much shocked as I was grateful for the complete support she offered me. We both understood that it would be a big sacrifice, but we also understood that it would be the first step to laying the foundation for the future. And the money would also come in handy for the wedding!

And so, after about two weeks, I was on a plane to Spain. After landing in Madrid, I took a seven-hour long train journey to Almeria, where I was met by Pablo's wife, Caro and one of our best friends – another member of our extended, international family – Gianmarco. As we embraced, I remember how wonderful it was to feel a sense of familiarity and security, even though I was miles away from home.

I was lucky enough to live in a flat only a couple of blocks away from Pablo and Caro, in the district of El Zapillo, in Almeria. And it didn't hurt either that it was only a five-minute walk away from the beach! El Zapillo would become my home away from home for the next eight months. There was a wonderful promenade with many cafés and restaurants open until late. After a long day at work, there was nothing better than to have a cup of coffee in the 'Paris' Café whilst admiring the beautiful sunset. The sound of the tide coming back and forth was magical.

In all honesty, with such picturesque conditions, it wasn't difficult to settle in at all. In fact, exchanging the stressful hustle and bustle of Lima for the zen-like ambiance of this seaside town was truly therapeutic.

After about three days of my arrival, I went for my interview, which fortunately went very well. I was going to work in the emergency department in the local hospital, doing day and night-time on calls. Because I was eager to get going and to save up some money, I asked my employer to roster me for as many on calls as she wanted; in Lima, as the 'newbie', I would have been expected to do so, no questions asked. Instead, to my surprise, my employer told me that I could only do a certain number of on calls per week and that I was entitled to 24 hours of rest after each on call! When I heard that, I couldn't believe it. I genuinely thought she had made some sort of mistake. I said, "Are you sure I don't have to work the next day?"

To this, she answered, "You can't, by law. You are legally entitled to 24 hours of no work." I was shocked. During all my years in Lima, I was never permitted to go home after an on call. Never. Everyone knew that this was simply *the way it was.* Furthermore, until you reached consultant level in Lima, you are expected to work 6–7 days per week, including on calls. So, as you can imagine, the conditions of my new job came as the most wonderful surprise! Essentially, I would be making much more money doing much less! A dream scenario which was unthinkable in Lima.

What I'm going to say next might seem like a joke or hyperbole, but it's not. During my on-call shifts in Almeria, I had a specific room, a desk and a chair to work from. To me, this was a luxury; I never had this in Lima. Over there, on calls were 'on-your-feet'. In the AE, there was only one small table with one chair that was typically used by the consultant. Everyone else was meant to be standing, seeing patients, writing using a clipboard or using the patient's bed for support and interacting with other staff members throughout the 12 or 24 hours of work.

Another very pleasant surprise was discovering that I could actually sleep more than one or two hours per night during my on calls! It was unbelievable! In Lima, until you were a last year trainee, you were simply not allowed to rest during your on calls. Once you reached last year, you were allowed to sleep for about two hours, as long as there wasn't any major problem in the AE. In Almeria, there was a special room where you could rest as long as there weren't any patients to attend to.

And finally, the food! What a difference! Whilst in Loazya Hospital I will never forget how I had to take my plate of food from out of the cupboard at lunch and dinner time. Basically, the cooks would prepare the food and leave all the served plates lined up within the cupboards of the kitchen. When it was lunch or dinnertime, you went to the kitchen and literally took out a random plate of food and ate it. It was usually cold by that time. In Almeria, there was a very nice cafeteria, with warm food!

These differences were not only striking but also revealing. It opened my eyes to workers' rights, a whole realm I had never even considered before and to the basic dignity that any employer must provide, not only by law but as a humane and moral requirement. In Lima, and in Peru in general, you are brought up to be grateful for whatever you have and to always remember that if you're not willing to do something at work, someone else will come along and do it instead. In other words, because you were 'expendable', you were best off not complaining too much. If you did so, you would soon be replaced by someone else. In Almeria, on the other hand, for the first time in my working life, I learned about 'worker's rights' and also to not be afraid of reminding my employer of them. It took me a long time to stop thinking that I 'had' to do something 'or else'. However, until I did so, I really struggled to say no' when asked to do something above and beyond my normal responsibilities.

As time went by, my job extended to doing on call work in different medical centres scattered throughout Almeria. This was quite interesting, because not only did it enable me to fully immerse myself into the local culture but also, while doing so, to discover the most common medical problems in this part of the world. It didn't take me too long to start discovering some very interesting differences.

There were several reasons for these differences. First of all, the tropical climate and the jungle regions of Peru increase the risk of infectious diseases. Second, poverty and poor sanitary conditions were major contributors to the increased prevalence of certain infections in Lima such as cholera, hepatitis, tuberculosis, HIV, salmonella, rotavirus (which causes diarrhoea in children), toxoplasmosis (cat-borne parasite), cysticercosis (parasite from undercooked meat), cytomegalovirus and malaria (contaminated water), amongst many others. Third, the lack of education – which usually goes hand-in-hand with poverty, mainly seen in the marginalised rural regions of Peru – greatly led (and still does) to lack of insight into the basic aspects of human health. As a direct consequence, in Peru, it wasn't uncommon to treat patients who had let chronic conditions, such as diabetes, progress for years without any formal management. Many of these patients lived in distant regions of Peru and by the time they managed to reach Lima, their medical conditions were extremely advanced. Therefore, as a student and junior doctor, I was accustomed to seeing the most extreme versions of many medical problems. It was very instructive for me but very unfortunate for the patient. For example, it was very common to see patients arrive to hospitals in Lima with end-stage diabetic neuropathies, end-stage peripheral vascular disease (requiring amputation), long-standing post-infectious complications (such as untreated epilepsy following a central nervous system infection), disseminated tuberculosis with multi-systemic complications, HIV-AIDS in end-stages, tertiary (neuro) syphilis, end-stage renal disease requiring dialysis, advanced and disabling rheumatoid arthritis and undiagnosed Parkinson's disease, amongst many others. And we mustn't forget the large cohort of patients with mental health disorders such as schizophrenia, bipolar, borderline personality disorder, depression, etc., that were either undiagnosed or very poorly treated. They too would arrive many times to the hospitals in Lima in a completely decompensated state, many times, requiring direct admission.

In Spain, on the other hand, I witnessed a much more effective system of primary prevention and because of that, there were much less cases of the previously described diseases. Having said this, Spain has its own medical epidemiology: cancers, dementia, strokes, lung cancer, hypercholesterolemia, cardiac problems, multiple sclerosis and Parkinson's disease, amongst others, are very common. In these cases, the main risk factors are not poverty and poor sanitary conditions but lifestyle risk factors such as smoking, alcohol intake, obesity and sedentary life.

Another difference between how medicine was practised in both countries was how much technology was available in Spain, as opposed to Peru. Although I already knew this, I had never experienced it first-hand. I wasn't prepared for what a significant difference in patient management and treatment it entailed. CT scans and MRI scans, for example, a true luxury in Lima, were routine in Almeria. Interestingly, part of my adaptation to this new and more modern way of practising medicine was to stop feeling guilty for requesting a CT or MRI! In Lima, there was a certain sense of disappointment from your superiors if you requested costly tests all the time. In fact, they even made you feel as if you 'weren't good enough' if you needed 'so much' radiological help!

One of the trademarks of Peruvian medicine is how much it's based on clinical skills. From day one of medical school, you are taught that history taking and the physical examination is at the core of the patient's diagnosis. You are taught that auxiliary investigations are just that: *auxiliary*, extra, non-essential. This medical ideology was very old and typically passed down from generation to generation. The old-school physicians, those who could diagnose everything by observing, touching, hearing, smelling and even tasting, were our idols. They were like medical oracles that we trusted above and beyond any auxiliary test. We all aspired to be like them. I remember being told by one of the most revered neurologists in Almenara Hospital that *a good neurologist is capable of interpreting a brain CT or an MRI. But an excellent one can predict, based on the physical examination and history, what he will see before looking at it.*

Those eight months in Almeria were as interesting as they were challenging. I learned a great deal about the culture and about a whole new way of practising medicine. Furthermore, during this time, I learned a great deal about myself, not only as a doctor but as a human being. My eyes were open to new realities, many of my preconceived ideas soon vanished away, and I started to take into consideration things that I had never given serious thought of before, such as the enforcement of my rights as a worker. My time in Almeria was proving to be a great experience, not only in medicine but also in life.

Eight months after arriving to Almeria, Lorena and I got married in Lima and then travelled back together to Almeria but not before going on a wonderful honeymoon to Italy and Morocco. Unfortunately, as soon as we returned to Almeria, I found out that I had lost my job. It was a terrible blow.

So, the next morning, I was knocking on all doors, searching for someone who would give me a job. After several failed attempts, I got a job in a very good hospital, the main one in Almeria. Once again, it was to work in the accident and emergency department whilst collaborating on the neurology ward; this was a wonderful opportunity because I still had not obtained my official licence to practise neurology in Spain. I was very happy with the opportunity.

I kept this job for about two years, but almost eight months into it, I had the opportunity to work as an ambulance doctor, transporting critically ill patients all throughout Andalucía. In hindsight, I think I shouldn't have taken this job; it was draining, emotionally and physically. Alternating on calls between the AE department in the hospital and the ambulance shift was exhausting. Nevertheless, I was able to do both jobs simultaneously for almost a year and a half. And, as if this wasn't enough, I decided to start my master's degree in Stem Cell Research!

In the midst of all this hard work, in August 2011, Lorena and I found out we were going to be parents! Lorena's due date was in March 2012. In July, I stopped working with the ambulance simply because I was exhausted. I couldn't keep doing two jobs without losing my mind! And, in November, my contract with the hospital expired, and unfortunately, they weren't able to extend it because the doctor I was covering for was returning after a long sabbatical. So, essentially, Lorena was three months from giving birth, and I didn't have a job.

About one week later, I was shocked to discover that Lorena and I would only have social security coverage for the first three months after my last day of work. So, essentially, if I didn't get a new job, our medical coverage would have ceased one month before Lorena's due date. I remember having terrible shingles on my arm and back about two weeks after that appointment! Few times in my life have I been under so much stress.

Apart from my own personal struggles, on a national level, Spain and the rest of Europe was starting to feel the effects of the looming economic crisis that would soon shake the world. Little by little, we started to notice how prices went up and salaries went down. Former colleagues of mine, who were able to hold on to their jobs, underwent a pay cut of about 35–50% between 2011 and 2013. It was such a very stressful time. It felt claustrophobic, as if every possible door and window around me was closing.

And then, something amazing happened; I got a call from a private hospital asking if I wanted a job! But the most amazing part of this was that I had dropped off my CV in this hospital about two years ago, when I came back from Lima and didn't have a job! I hadn't heard anything from them until now, one month before Valentina was born! I was so happy and relieved that I slept for 24 hours straight.

For the next month, I worked practically every day. But that didn't matter. I had a job! On 26 March, despite hours of labour, Lorena had to undergo a caesarean section because Valentina's body wasn't aligned for a natural delivery. About one hour later, our beautiful daughter was born! I remember how her huge eyes where wide open, staring at me, as if to say, "So, it was you who I've been hearing for the past nine months!" I carried Valentina in my arms for four hours straight, in a dark room, waiting for Lorena to come out of recovery. As I had her in my arms, she never stopped staring at me! All I can remember thinking was 'please don't cry!'

With Valentina in our lives, our family was complete (although we eventually got Mathilda, our family cockapoo two years ago, and Valentina would kill me if she finds out I didn't include her!). My personal life was what I had always aspired it to be. It was my professional one that was seriously suffering.

The crisis in Europe was bleak. First Greece, then Portugal, then Spain started to fall. Soon, each and every country in Europe would feel the profound effects of the economic crisis. While the unemployment rate shot up, so did the suicide rate. Salaries plummeted for all health care workers, who were probably the only people who actually could hang on to a job. It was very harsh.

Towards the beginning of 2013, I started to feel like the situation was unsustainable. My salary had decreased and I wasn't able to save any money at all. After two days of receiving my pay-check, practically nothing was left; all the money was eaten up by the monthly expenses. Something had to be done.

At that point, Lorena and I knew that we wouldn't be staying much longer in Spain, despite our love for it and despite how grateful we were to all the opportunities it had offered us. However, the overall situation had drastically changed. The world wasn't the same anymore and people were flocking either back to their original countries or emigrating for a second and even a third time. Things were so bad that the majority of employers offered only one or two-day contracts, to work 'as-and-when', without benefits; one day you had a job and the next day, you didn't anymore.

So, we started exploring options in the UK, even though we knew it wouldn't be easy, mainly because I didn't have a licence to practise medicine there, Lorena didn't speak English and we had hardly any savings! Nevertheless, after discovering that there were several interesting job offers, we decided to move forward. It was an uphill battle, I confess. We had to obtain a visa for Lorena, the GMC licence and save as much money as we could for the moving expenses. And all this, *before* the official interview.

Finally, once all these documents were arranged and the GMC provided me with the consultant licence, I was now available to officially apply for jobs in the UK. That was the next big chapter in our lives, which I will describe further ahead in the book.

Fatima

It was about 3 am when my phone rang. "Doctor, there's a patient you need to urgently see. She's a 19-year-old pregnant girl."

I jumped out of bed, not knowing where I was headed to. This was only my third on call shift since arriving to Almeria, about four weeks before. I had no idea how things ran here – I was just finding my bearings.

I quickly got changed, hung my stethoscope around my neck (which I hadn't done in a long time! In neurology, we usually don't listen to people's hearts or lungs!) and ran out to the ambulance that was waiting outside the emergency room. As I was running, I wondered, *You're a newly qualified neurologist! What on earth are you doing attending to a 19-year-old pregnant patient! In fact, what on earth are you doing in Almeria!*

But it was too late to turn back. The ambulance door flung open as the driver told me, "Hop in, Doctor, we're leaving now!"

As we drove through the empty streets, the nurse traveling with me gave me a quick summary of the case. "She's 19 years old; she's 29 weeks pregnant, and it seems like she's bleeding."

After listening to this, I asked, "But why doesn't she go to the emergency room so that a gynaecologist sees her?"

"Well, she can't do that because she is detained in the port of Almeria." This was the answer from the ambulance driver. "That's where we're going now." To this, he added, "And plus, we received the initial phone call from the police who is with her at the scene. They have her in custody."

My mind was spinning. I was half asleep, traveling in a speeding ambulance to see a pregnant girl who was in police custody, in the port of Almeria at 3 am! *Good start, Carlo* is all I could think of!

After about ten minutes, we arrived. As I stepped out of the ambulance, I could hear chanting, which really threw me off. Chanting at 3 am, in the port? What on earth was going on? As I started to run towards the dock – in the direction of the chanting – I started to see in the distance a huge cage-like structure. As I got nearer, I realised that the chanting was coming from hundreds of people, locked up in this makeshift jail.

I was utterly baffled. Very soon, one of the Guardia Civil (policemen) came up to me and asked me, "Are you the doctor?"

"Yes," I said (a bit hesitantly, I have to admit!).

"The patient is in there. Come with me. I'll take you inside to see her."

As I followed him into the jail – which had no doors or walls, just hundreds of metal bars lined up side to side – I saw hundreds of people. Some were sitting on the floor, others were standing. Some were holding their babies and breastfeeding them and others were sustaining the elderly.

And they were all chanting in unison. It was a surreal experience.

They were all Moroccan immigrants that had travelled in rafts from their country (which is about four hours away in ferry but days away by raft; that is, if you survive), trying to enter Spain through the southern border. They weren't successful. As soon as their little rafts approached the port, Spanish border patrol seized them and immediately incarcerated them, labelling them as 'illegal' immigrants.

As I followed the police, my heart sunk. I couldn't believe what I was experiencing. A great sense of anger came over me. I was horrified by this inhumane scene.

I finally reached my patient: a terrified young girl, pale to the bone and trembling from head to toe. Luckily, she spoke a bit of English and French. As I kneeled down to see her eye-to-eye, I asked her, "What's your name?"

"Fatima," she replied.

"Okay, and does your belly hurt you? Have you been bleeding?" I asked.

"Yes, since yesterday; since we arrived here."

"Well then, let's get you up and into the ambulance. I'm taking you to the hospital," I said. As I held her hand, I noticed that she had the number 21145 written on the interior of her wrist. That shook me to the core. *Just like Auschwitz,* I kept thinking to myself. As I turned around, I noticed that everyone had a number written on their wrists.

To my surprise, the policeman, when he heard my intention to take her away in the ambulance, aggressively told me that I couldn't do that because she was in custody and that I had to 'fix the problem' here. "What? Are you crazy? I'm going with her and if you want, you can follow me in your patrol car. I don't care."

So, I took Fatima by the arm and slowly walked her to the ambulance. Interestingly, the policeman didn't even move. He just looked at me walk away. As we were heading off, he told the ambulance driver that he would send another patrolman to the hospital first thing in the morning to bring her back.

Off we went. I rode in the back of the ambulance with her. "Don't worry. Everything's going to be fine. I'll help you once we get to the hospital. I'll tell you how to escape," I told her. Her eyes suddenly opened wide, looking at me steadily as if she didn't know how to react. "Don't worry, I know what to do. You won't have to go back."

As soon as we arrived at the hospital, I took her to the obstetric AE, where she was assessed and admitted for further management. I was pleased because I knew that at least she would spend the upcoming days in a warm bed, with warm food and with people who would take care of her and her baby.

In the meantime, I was able to persuade the social worker to find her a place to go after she had her baby. There was no way I was going to let her go back, especially with a newborn baby. In the ambulance, although I told Fatima that I would help her escape the hospital, I soon realised that I could never do this, not because I wasn't willing to but because there was no way I would help her escape in the medical condition she was in. Nevertheless, that didn't keep me from pulling all the strings I could in order to secure her a safe place to go.

Five days later, she had a beautiful baby boy. Sadly, neither her husband, sisters or parents were with her, as they were all incarcerated (or perhaps even deported). Nevertheless, she and her baby were safe. And that was enough for me.

I never saw her again.

Francois

Roughly towards the end of 2011, I was working in a hospital called Santa Rosa, one of the oldest hospitals in Almeria. It was located in a rough neighbourhood and it was common to see patients with gunshot and stab wounds, domestic violence and other violent crimes. That much I was aware of before starting to work there. However, what I wasn't aware of, was the huge amount of drug-related violence in that area. It was astonishing. Very soon, I would learn why.

One Friday night, at about 11 pm, I get a call from the nurse who says, "Carlo, you'll need to come to the AE soon because there's a policeman bringing in a drug dealer." I was brought aback, wondering why I – the doctor on call - had to deal with a drug-dealer?

"Does he have any medical problem?" I asked.

"I think he has abdominal pain," she replied.

It all seemed strange to me, to say the least. A drug dealer with abdominal pain? Oh well, there wasn't too much time to think about it.

So, I turned up to the AE and saw a handcuffed young man, no more than 25 years old, surrounded by two armed policemen. His name was Francois. According to the policemen, he had been spotted trying to enter illegally the country through the shores of Almeria. Once in custody, he started complaining of severe abdominal pain and demanded to see a doctor. Fair enough, I thought. At least there seems to be a medical 'problem' that justifies his arrival to the AE.

Several things came to mind as a potential cause. Maybe he had a viral infection or maybe he was just constipated? After all, travelling in the middle of the night, in a makeshift raft from the coast of Algeria to the coast of Almeria could have brought about a number of different medical issues.

As I was palpating his abdomen, apart from noticing that he had severe pain, I also felt his skin very hot. The nurse quickly took his temperature and noted that it was 41 C. Something was very wrong. Appendicitis? Peritonitis?

I requested an abdominal X-ray and a complete blood count. The former showed signs of some sort of raging infection with a white blood count more than 30, when the normal amount is up to 5 or 6. But it was the X-ray that floored me. I placed the X-ray up to the light (yes, 'old school' style! No computers!) and saw at least 30 little sphere-like structures scattered throughout his bowels. They were all perfectly round, identical in shape and size. *What on earth was that?* I thought to myself. One of the policemen, who was standing behind me and who caught a glimpse of the X-ray, suddenly says, "It's cocaine, Doc. I've seen that before."

I was speechless. Completely baffled. Francois was smuggling cocaine over the southern coast of Spain, by transporting dozens of packed cocaine balls in his bowels. Unbelievably, even as the X-ray showed the evidence, he strongly denied it. Why? Well, as the policemen explained to me, they can only keep him in custody for 24 hours and if by that time he did 'pass them', he would be able to go free. So, François knew that if he could hold it in for 24 hours, he would be off the hook. The other policeman educated me on how these dealers do this. "They ingest these balls – as many as they can, because they get paid per ball – one or two hours before getting on the raft and then head off."

Even though Francois knew that he had a chance if he didn't pass them within the first 24 hours, that was easier said than done. The abdominal pain coupled with the very high fever pointed to an acute abdominal problem, possibly a surgical one.

So, we rushed him to another hospital where there was a surgical team waiting to assess him. On the way over, I thought to myself, *maybe one of the cocaine 'balls' exploded and has damaged the bowel walls?* It seemed like a probable cause. I honestly couldn't think of any other alternative.

I think that the decision to take him directly to theatre didn't take more than 10 to 15 minutes. He was going for an exploratory laparotomy due to the high suspicion of cocaine-induced peritonitis or perhaps, even worse. Eventually, after about four or five hours of surgery, François was taken to the ITU with the post-surgical diagnosis of large bowel perforation with areas of ischemia (infarction) and evidence of multiple 'foreign objects', i.e., 'cocaine balls' in the peritoneum. A large part of his bowels was resected, requiring a colostomy.

Even though he survived the surgery, he died only after 72 hours due to ongoing mesenteric ischemia (poor blood flow to the bowel) and severe sepsis. He was in his mid-twenties.

I later found out that he was going to receive only 300 euros for this job. Imagine the degree of desperation a young man has to feel in order to risk his life for 300 euros. As a doctor, my only job was to help him as much as I could, not to judge him. However, as a human being, I could only feel sadness for a lost soul who lost his life unnecessarily.

Lucas

As I was walking towards the entrance of the hospital, Paco, the ambulance driver said, "Good morning, Carlo. We're going to Seville."

"What do you mean? Now? For what?" I asked (hoping he was joking).

"Well, there's a patient in critical condition in the ITU that needs a special type of surgery that can only be done in Virgen del Rocio Hospital in Seville."

At that time, I was working in an ambulance service transporting critical patients. I was accustomed to taking patients from Almeria to Granada or to Malaga, which were about two or three hours away. However, Seville was a whopping five hours away and we were in the middle of summer, at a scorching 40 degrees. Going to Seville implied sitting in a hot and humid ambulance for a total of ten hours. But work was work, and it had to be done, despite the fact I wanted to run back home!

Lucas – my patient – was 38 years old and until his admission to the ITU had led a perfectly normal and healthy life. Little did he know, he had a malignant brain tumour slowly taking over his brain. According to the notes, he had been admitted to the hospital about two weeks ago due to persistent headaches, disequilibrium, blurred vision, episodes of disorientation and vomiting. The CT scan done in the AE was unquestionable; a tumour had emerged in the back of his brain (in the cerebellum, the part of the brain that controls our balance, amongst other things), next to the ventricular system, which is the passageway (like a drainage system) of the cerebrospinal fluid (CSF), which surrounds and protects the brain. Because it was blocking the normal CSF flow, this was leading to an increased amount of pressure. This was extremely dangerous; it was potentially lethal.

The ICU doctors had managed to stabilise him as best as possible, but unfortunately, without surgery, the tumour would continue to grow and to compress the vital structures. That particular procedure was offered in Seville (and also in Madrid). Hence, we were off to Seville!

Seville is one of the most picturesque cities in Andalusia, indeed one of my favourites. It's majestic, royal, historic and colourful, full of lively people and wonderful food. It hosts the Virgen del Rocio Hospital, one of the best in all of Spain. It's always a pleasure to visit Seville, however, going in summer is not recommended: temperatures can reach 44–45 degrees centigrade sometimes. In fact, because it's so hot, the majority of businesses close and their owners take vacations in Malaga or Almeria, for example (where it's 'only' 35-38 degrees!).

But this time, I wasn't going for pleasure. Lucas was seriously ill and in need for life-saving surgery.

The ambulance I worked in was like a mini-ICU. It was specially equipped for transporting critical patients. In fact, in order to work in it, I received pretty intense training. I was pretty confident with all the neurological emergencies but needed a crash course for all the rest!

Just getting Lucas into the ambulance was quite an accomplishment. He was intubated and hooked to several IV lines with drips containing strong medications such as noradrenaline. He laid with his head facing the driver's seat whilst several IV lines dangled from each side of his body. The gurney was locked to the floor so that he couldn't move side to side, and I had a small space to sit down right behind his head.

I was completely oblivious that my ride to Seville that day would deeply touch me; that it would make me reflect upon life in a way I hadn't before.

As I was somewhat trapped in between the back of the driver's seat and Lucas' head, I couldn't avoid visualising myself in Lucas' place. It was one of the most sobering moments of my life. Five long hours of focusing on the unconscious face of this 38-year-old young man, who, by no fault of his own, found himself on the verge of dying. *That could be me* is all I could think. *Why him and not me?* was the uncomfortable question that kept springing to mind.

Even if he survived, he would invariably have brain damage. The question was: how much and to what extent it would affect him? Would it be serious enough to remove vital memories of his childhood? Would he become oblivious to his dreams, aspirations and secrets? Would he be able to recognise himself in the mirror or would he be condemned to living in a 'foreign' body? Would he recognise his wife, children, parents, siblings and friends? Or would they all be unknown 'invaders' of his personal space? Would his personality and behaviour change? Would he ever be able to return to work?

As our journey continued, all these questions and indeed many more kept coming to mind. Sadly, I couldn't answer any of them. The only thing I knew for sure was that Lucas was in a complete state of limbo and that his life, as he once knew it, was a coin toss away from vanishing forever.

Another question popped to mind, one that was haunting to think about: if he was going to die, would he have been satisfied with the short life he had led? Had he had the chance to miraculously rise, fully cured, would he do anything different? I asked myself these questions: if I could go back in time, would I change anything I had done in my life until then? More so, if I were to suddenly change places with Lucas, how would Lorena, Valentina, my extended family and friends remember me? Had I given them enough reasons to be proud of me? Had I told them enough times that I loved them, needed them and missed them?

At that very moment, as the ambulance rushed along the bumpy road and my eyes focused on Lucas' face, my career suddenly stopped being that all-mighty driving force in my life. My love for neurology and the deep passion it exerted within me suddenly seemed to move aside, creating a well-deserved place in my heart and in my mind for feelings and thoughts that had been displaced for too long.

At the end of the day, when our time on this planet is up, the *only* thing that will matter is how our loved ones remember us. Personal success and academic and professional success are undeniably important and worth developing; however, in the grand scheme of things, their relevance pales in comparison with the relationships and the experiences we could have built with our loved ones. If we live on through the memories of those who knew us, how do you want to be remembered? How do you want to live-on after passing?

Ever since that day, I have tried to balance my personal and professional life as best as possible. When my career starts to over bound my personal life, I can easily bring it back into equilibrium asking myself the following questions: *What will have a more transcendent effect: reading this scientific paper on a subject that will probably be rebutted in a year or turning off my computer and hugging my wife and daughter?* And just like that, I'm back on track.

In my opinion, everyone has to have a *balancing* question that he or she can recur to in times of doubt. A *perspective* question that immediately relocates our priorities and re-centres our efforts and emotions.

As I was travelling back from Seville, I had one last question. It stemmed, in part due to the ten-hour period of deep and unexpected introspection and also in part due to the fact that my ambulance work was only on the weekends. The last question was: 'Should I keep volunteering for on call shifts to work in the ambulance or should I pack it up and simply work from Monday to Friday?'

I think you might suspect the answer! Of course, I said goodbye to the ambulance and 'hello' to weekends with family. The best decision I made in a very long time. After all, I had run away from seven-day working jobs in Peru; why on earth would I go back to it? That was it for me.

Norwich

By the end of 2012, for numerous reasons, Lorena and I were convinced that we couldn't stay in Spain anymore. The European economic crisis felt like an invisible straitjacket, squeezing the life out of the whole country. On the other hand, from a professional point of view, both of us felt like we needed a change. Essentially, as we looked to the future, we didn't think that Spain was in our cards.

And so, we started to consider other options. I remember how we sat down one night with a pencil and paper in hand and started to write down all the possible countries we could look into. Initially, the UK seemed impossible because Lorena didn't speak English, but nevertheless, it was on the list. We had Italy and Sweden. However, Italy was not much better than Spain at the time and in Sweden, although I had a friend who worked as a paediatric neurosurgeon on the Italian border, she told me I would have to undergo a huge amount of extra training before I could even consider it.

I had always considered the UK as an amazing country to practise medicine in; however, it always seemed a bit difficult to access, for several reasons. Given the fact that my neurology degree was from a non-EU country, I was aware that it was going to be very difficult to get it recognised in the UK. And on the other hand, as I mentioned before, Lorena didn't speak English. So, although the UK was an amazing option, we saw it as a very high mountain to climb.

Nevertheless, we decided to give it a shot. After thinking about it long and hard, we thought that the sacrifice and effort to get to the UK would pay off in the long run. Once the decision was made, I embarked on looking for every job offer out there. There was a very interesting job as a stroke consultant in James Paget Hospital (JPUH), which I thought was an excellent opportunity for me because, despite not being for a neurologist, it was for managing stroke patients, which I had done during my neurology training in Peru. I found this interesting; in the UK, 'stroke medicine' is not part of the neurology training program; it is a separate speciality, one that historically stemmed from geriatrics, as the majority of patients with strokes are elderly. This was an interesting avenue to explore for me. It enabled me to work in the closest field to neurology as I could.

After Lore and I decided to go all in with this option, a painstaking bureaucratic journey started! I think it took me a good five months to collect, translate, submit, correct and resubmit all the necessary documents to be accredited by GMC (General Medical Council) to work as a doctor in the UK. The amount of money (which we didn't have!) that we invested in official translations was tremendous. But alas, it was done. Once I received the official GMC stamp of approval, I was free to formally apply to job offers in the UK.

Although I had the option of looking at any potential job offer in the UK, for me, the stroke consultant job in JPUH was the most appealing, not only because I was comfortable treating stroke patients but also because it brought me as close as possible to neurology. After sending my CV to JPUH, I was very pleased to receive a prompt reply, requesting a face-to-face interview. A date was agreed: 12 June 2013.

Until 11 June 2013, one day before my job interview in James Paget University Hospital, I had never stepped foot in the UK. It won't come as a surprise to the reader that one of my strongest impressions came as soon as I stepped out of the airport; I was welcomed by heavy rain and chilling gusts of wind, despite being in the middle of summer! However, this was my fault! I should have expected it! Everyone knows just how unpredictable the weather in the UK is. Anyways, I took it as my first valuable lesson!

As I stood on the train platform wearing just a short-sleeved shirt and a pair of jeans, I sincerely had no idea how I was going to get to JPUH. I had a rough idea but no clear directions. When I asked for some help, I was shocked by how little I understood, despite knowing how to speak English! I had a similar problem in Spain; the Spanish I spoke in Peru was significantly different from what I spoke in Spain; there was a large number of words, expressions and meanings that I had to 're-learn'. Whilst a very kind gentleman was giving me directions, I discovered that my American-style English was significantly different from the British English and that I would have to adapt very quickly if I was going to survive in the UK!

The next shock – which by this time was psychologically affecting me – came from not understanding a word of what was being said on the loudspeaker inside the train! At that point, I told myself:

You've done pretty good so far, just take a seat and drink your coffee! The interview is still tomorrow, so if you get lost, you'll still have a lot of time to find your way!

Once I arrived in Cambridge, I felt pretty good with myself! I knew that there was only one more stop before I got to Norwich. Little did I know, I still had to take one last train ride from Norwich to Great Yarmouth.

Well, by the time I arrived in Great Yarmouth, it was 11 pm. As soon as I stepped off the train, I noticed that the hospital was not in walking distance but that I had to take a taxi or a bus there! Remember, this was the first time I was in the UK, let alone Great Yarmouth! Eventually, I found a taxi and reached the hospital. Finally! What a relief!

Fortunately, the following day, despite being exhausted, my interview went pretty well. I was so pleased! I called Lorena right after and told her, "I think it went okay. You might need to start practising your English!" After a couple of days, I received a phone call to tell me that I had the job! And so, our journey to the UK officially began. This was going to be the fourth country I lived in!

On 13 September, we arrived in Norwich. I was due to start on the 27th. Unfortunately, by the time we arrived, all the flats that we had lined up as options had been either rented or sold. So, we had to stay in a hotel whilst we looked for other options. We found a place after about ten days. The only problem was that we had no furniture! All of our things were arriving in 15 days! So, until it all arrived, we slept on an inflatable mattress. You can imagine how 'comfortable' it was to do that, especially with an 18-month-old child! More so, the flat we obtained didn't have chairs or tables either, so we had to eat on the floor! Another fun experiment with an 18-month-old! (not recommended!)

Another major difficulty we had was that we had no car. Right before leaving Almeria, a 'friend' who was a mechanic offered to buy our car and gave us a down payment of 500 euros two days before we left and told us he would send us the remaining amount two weeks later. Well, that money never arrived. Our so-called 'friend' stole our car. We were counting on that money, so suddenly discovering that it was never coming, added extra pressure.

During the following year, I took the bus from the Norwich train station to Great Yarmouth. Eventually, after paying off the credit card bills and other things, I was able to start saving up a bit in order to buy a car. When I was able to finally buy it, I had to learn how to drive again! I had never driven a car with the steering wheel on the 'other' side! So, little by little, my brain had to adjust to this new format.

These were only a few of the many challenges, sacrifices and adjustments we all had to make. However, as time went by, we settled in little by little. As I write this chapter, Valentina is nine years old and speaks English and Spanish (and a bit of French) better than I do! She's in a wonderful school and has many friends. And Lorena, apart from having also a great group of friends, she passed her GCSE English this year. I have to also mention a particular accomplishment which I am extremely proud of: she passed her UK driver's licence. Before coming to the UK, she did not know how to drive; however, with a huge amount of dedication, she did it. Although we have been married for eleven years and we know each other for 14, her resilience, dedication and capacity to overcome goals never stop to amaze me. I can see that resilience and mental strength in Valentina and it fills my heart with joy and admiration.

Joyce

For three months, Joyce had attended AE numerous times for recurrent abdominal pain. Each time, she would be examined and undergo a series of blood tests to rule out infections and other possible causes. Each time, everything was negative. On one occasion, the surgeon assessed her to see if there was any evidence of appendicitis or peritonitis; however, he found no evidence of either diagnosis. All blood and urine cultures were consistently negative, her abdominal X-rays showed constipation (but no obstruction), and she was never feverish. She did mention, however, that her menstrual periods had become more irregular during the previous six months but that her GP had assured her that it was probably due to 'polycystic ovaries', which was somewhat 'expected' in a overweight and hirsute 23-year-old female.

And so, after each visit to the AE, Joyce would return home disappointed by the fact that 'nothing was wrong', despite the fact that the pain she felt was very 'real'. The frustration only grew more intense every time someone told her that 'it's probably due to anxiety or stress'.

On the background of all this, Joyce had been developing very subtle behavioural changes that had been picked up by her partner and her family; however, once again, it was put down to being 'overworked and stressed'.

As time went by, all these symptoms progressively worsened. However, because all the examinations were normal and the behavioural changes were 'atypical' or 'unexpected' for such a young patient – who obviously doesn't have dementia – no further investigations were done and she was left as simply being 'too anxious'. Unfortunately, this scenario is all too common; patients who present with subjective symptoms such as pain, dizziness, light-headedness, etc., without any objective explanation, i.e., no abnormal blood test or radiological assessment, are quickly labelled as being 'anxious' or to be 'making it up' ('it's all in your head' is a frequent pseudo 'explanation').

In neurology, one of the most challenging aspects of diagnosing a patient is trying to ground the subjectivity of their symptoms: is it coming from a physical source or not? After being married for more than eleven years with a psychologist, I have learned darn well to avoid asking 'is it real or not' because *of course* subjective symptoms are real *for the patient!* The fact that they don't have a physical source doesn't make them unreal or 'made up'. *They are as real as they are experienced by the patient.* Having said this, in my world, if a patient with dizziness, blurred vision, light-headedness, vertigo, headaches, etc. has no obvious cause – either on blood tests, scans or physical examination – it rapidly leads me to think that perhaps, there's something either not neurological going on or that, indeed, there might be an underlying psychological problem that needs assessing.

However – and this is an emphatic 'however'– all this depends on *the patient.* The worse offence a doctor can commit is to marginalise or to inappropriately 'label' a patient just because his or her symptoms simply don't 'fit' into a specific diagnostic 'box'. Put more bluntly: just because a doctor doesn't know what's wrong with a patient, doesn't mean that the patient *doesn't have a problem*. After three months of negative results, Joyce was rapidly heading towards that ill fate.

One night, as Joyce attended AE yet again with abdominal pain, she was lucky enough to come across an excellent colleague of mine who didn't accept the 'anxiety' diagnosis and decided to request an abdominal CT scan. To everyone's surprise, Joyce had what appeared to be a large – and mostly benign – ovarian tumour! That *was* the source of abdominal pain! Finally!

Not long after, a series of serologic tumour markers for malignancy came back negative and an ovarian resection was scheduled to be done when possible.

But what about the ever-growing behavioural changes? What was to be made of them? Were they, as everyone had assumed, simply secondary to anxiety or could the ovarian tumour have something to do with this, even though it might seem like a ludicrous suggestion? The short answer is that it could!

Before I explain the association, let me give you a brief description of what Joyce's behavioural changes actually implied. Initially, she displayed signs of irritability, getting into frequent arguments at home and with her children. As time went by, this irritability would overflow into bouts of aggressiveness and of verbal insults, frequently accompanied by insulting gesticulations Almost one month before the ovarian tumour was detected, sudden bouts of inexplicable crying and laughter started to occur on a daily basis. All of this was completely out of character. According to her family, she was one of the most gentle and loving teachers in her school; she had a stable relationship with her partner and always visited her parents on the weekends. So, this was the most unexpected metamorphosis of character and personality.

What could an ovarian tumour (which turned out to be a benign tumour called a teratoma) have to do with behaviour disorders of such nature? Psychiatric conditions such as bipolar or borderline personality disorder could have easily been put forth as reasonable aetiologies for such a dramatic metamorphosis. Well, it turns out that such psychiatric-like symptoms can be the prodrome to a very rare type of encephalitis (inflammation of the brain) called limbic encephalitis, which is triggered by pathological autoantibodies produced by an underlying tumour. In other words, the tumour produces antibodies that damage the limbic system, the part of brain that primarily controls our behaviours and memories.

I came to meet Joyce after the colleague who had requested the CT asked me for my opinion regarding the odd behaviour. With the background of the teratoma, it became relatively easy to put the pieces together. What was needed was a smoking gun: a positive antibody test in blood and/or in her cerebrospinal fluid. Not long after, there was indeed a positive result for a specific antibody, making the diagnosis conclusive. After the teratoma resection and several courses of plasma exchange (a special treatment to remove the damaging antibodies from her bloodstream), she started to display an impressive improvement in her behaviour. Unfortunately, although the aggressiveness, irritability and emotional lability greatly improved, her short-term memory was markedly damaged, leading her to forget things that had happened only five or six hours before.

She had survived but had lost her short-term memory in the process. What do you think about this? Put yourself in her position for a moment: imagine that at the age of 23 you could no longer form short-term memories. Imagine that although you could remember everything from your past, you gravely struggle to recall anything that happened to you in the immediate past. It's as if Joyce had suddenly acquired Alzheimer's disease, which causes the same pattern of memory loss.

Sadly, upon reflection, one cannot avoid wondering what would have happened to Joyce had she been given the benefit of the doubt from the onset.

Limbic encephalitis is a non-infectious type of encephalitis, which if treated very early on, can lead to a remarkable recovery. Very sadly, this was not the case for Joyce. Although she survived, she was permanently damaged. That scar would be nearly impossible to remove.

Let me finish this story with a word of advice for the junior doctors that may be reading this book. You might come across ten cases like Joyce, nine of which will end up being due to 'anxiety and stress' but one – *the one* – will not be. *That's the one* you cannot afford to miss. That *one* is a whole and unique life. The only way of doing that is treating all of your patients with the same degree of interest, dedication and reasonable doubt. And if by some sad turn of events, *that one* escapes you despite your best efforts, at least you'll know you did as much as you could. Because, believe me, living with regrets in medicine is deeply painful.

This profession is too long, too complex and too unpredictable to assume that you can prevent all unfortunate cases such as that of Joyce. To assume the contrary would be extremely naïve and quite frankly, irrational. As a young doctor, your experiences – *all of them*: good and bad – will shape your decision-making for your future cases. As you move along in your career, if you learn from your mistakes and remember your successes, chances are, that *that one* patient won't escape you. You owe it to all the potential Joyces out there that undoubtedly *will* cross your path at some point. And that, my dear unknown friend, will not only make you a better doctor but also a better human being.

This case is a great example for how vital medical research is. Ten or fifteen years ago, in Peru, Spain and the UK, there was very little – if at all – information regarding autoimmune encephalitis. Many of the necessary assays to test for the damaging antibodies were just being developed and there was no available serologic test that could certify the diagnosis. Furthermore, because little was known about the condition, it wasn't on the differential diagnoses list of most physicians. Consequently, many people went undiagnosed.

Nowadays, however, the literature regarding many autoimmune neurological conditions – including encephalitis – has exploded. New antibodies are constantly being discovered and subsequently being linked to specific clinical conditions, which weren't formally recognised before. Evidence of a specific antibody in the bloodstream can be the smoking gun for an elusive diagnosis and possibly can open therapeutic avenues. With the advent of new diagnostic methods, what we used to consider as a 'rare' or an 'unknown' condition has gradually become a fairly common one.

Essentially, it wasn't that the condition was 'rare', it was simply 'underdiagnosed'.

This is one of the marvels of research: unveiling a hidden problem, giving it a name and treating it accordingly.

Unfortunately, in developing countries such as Peru, even though clinicians might be aware of these new advances, it is not uncommon – in fact, it's usually the rule – that the technology isn't available. I remember the feeling as I read through sophisticated American and European medical journals whilst thinking, *what's the use? None of this is available here.* That is one of the most frustrating feelings a doctor can have: knowing how to help but not being able to. Reading things such as genetic testing, sophisticated biopsy and serologic assays, new medications and even for that matter MRIs felt like a completely different world from where I was. I longed for the day I could practise medicine in a country – like the UK, for example – with a huge research infrastructure and all the technological tools one could desire. I can do that now, and the feeling is remarkable

George

"The last two years of our lives have been complete hell. For some reason, George just changed. We have no idea why. He was perfectly fine before that. He used to work in a cinema since the age of 21 until about 24. But then, everything changed. He never went back to normal. He's been getting worse by the day. Yesterday, he turned 26 and he didn't even know it."

As George's tear-eyed father spoke these words, I gazed over to his son, observing a very skinny and dishevelled young man, who displayed a series of irregular facial automatisms, waving hand gesticulations, wandering eyes and constant fidgeting in his seat. His nails and teeth were markedly yellow, his hair was uncombed; he had not shaved in at least 3–4 weeks, his cloths hung as if they were 2–3 sizes too large, and his shoelaces were twirled up in many knots as if it had been done by a child.

"He wasn't like this, Doctor. He's unrecognisable," his mother told me, as she caught my gaze. "He even had a steady girlfriend," she added.

I tried to speak to George directly, but he wasn't able to answer me in complete sentences; he simply repeated monosyllables such as 'no' or 'yes' whilst he shook his head.

Occasionally, he would interrupt the conversation by saying something that had nothing to do with the matter, such as 'I didn't want to go' or 'I listen to music'. I tried to get him to follow the line of conversation, but it was impossible. He would gaze off in another direction as if no one else was in the room with him.

"You see? This is how he's been for the past two years. Things are getting worse by the day. One year ago, he could still talk to us, but now, it's nearly impossible to get through to him."

His mum, who mentioned this, also added that he was gradually losing the capacity to do many things that he was perfectly able to do before, such as getting dressed, making decisions, planning for the future, taking a bath, etc. He needed help for all of these things.

"Has anyone investigated him for potential causes?" I asked. There was a unanimous 'No' in reply, from everyone in the room, except of course, from George himself. This was a dreadful situation; he had slipped through the crack of the system. The only diagnosis he had received was 'psychological/mental health issues' and was prescribed an antidepressant, which he never took. From that point on, nothing else was done.

As a neurologist, I'm pretty accustomed to seeing patients that have been 'lost to follow up' or simply forgotten or discharged because no formal diagnosis was obtained, i.e., so-called 'idiopathic' cases or as I like to call them, 'neurological orphans'. In all honesty, I am quite keen on undertaking these cases, as they are both challenging and fulfilling for all parties, but in George's case, there seemed to be a tragic element to it, that laid out his dreadful fate even if I was able to come up with a formal diagnosis. His case seemed to have surpassed the threshold of hope.

Nevertheless, I said, "Okay, let's start at the beginning. Tell me everything, from start to finish." Even if the final diagnosis would, in all likelihood, turn out to be irreversible and possibly even lethal, George and his family deserved to know what was going on. So, let me tell you the story of George.

One of the first symptoms he presented at the very beginning of his condition, whilst he was still able to function independently and work in the cinema, was an obsession for drinking large quantities of water in very short periods of time. For example, he could drink up to four or five pints of water in 15 minutes (the medical term for this is 'polydipsia'). This would be done many times a day, on a daily basis. Obviously, this led him to go to the toilet 15–20 times per day. When bottled water was not available, he would directly start drinking out of the tap. After about one month of this behaviour, he had some blood test done to assess if his polydipsia was being caused by something organic (such as a brain tumour or perhaps, diabetes) and if, on the other hand, it had led to complications, such as changes in his sodium levels, which, if severe enough, can cause seizures and even death. The CT scan did not show evidence of a brain tumour and all the blood investigations were essentially normal.

At this stage, because the initial tests did not reveal any obvious cause, he was told that it's 'psychological' and that he needed to take an antidepressant. And so, off he went with a new prescription and a diagnosis of 'psychogenic polydipsia'. Sadly, he didn't receive an appointment to see a mental health practitioner for another year. This is the sad state of affairs for many patients in the UK. Despite the remarkable service that the NHS provides – indeed, a worldwide example of social health care – the mental health services are markedly overwhelmed by the huge number of patients. Consequently, patients with mental health problems are typically not seen for months on end.

Having said this, in the end, George turned out not to have a mental health problem, *despite presenting as one.* Nevertheless, had he received an appointment sooner, I'm pretty sure that his real diagnosis would have been picked up sooner. This is another very frequent yet unfortunate situation: patients might be labelled as having disease 'X' or 'Y' and immediately get placed in a 'diagnostic basket'. This is a major problem, especially when the current health care system is set up to see patients with 'specific' problems. If problem 'X' or 'Y' requires help from service 'M' or 'N', for example, which are already overwhelmed, then that patient will not be seen for a very long time. However, perhaps problem 'X' or 'Y' are 'associated with other conditions' that are not typically seen by service 'M' or 'N'; this patient might benefit from seeing, for example, another service, like 'N' or 'G' in the meantime. This detour 'bypasses' the long waiting list – decentralising the process – and potentially leads to an earlier diagnosis and a treatment. I suspect that if George's 'psychogenic' polydipsia (problem 'X', for example) would have been assessed by other specialities – such as neurology or endocrinology – whilst waiting for the mental health assessment, he would have probably received a diagnosis sooner. The problem was that he was labelled as 'psychogenic' and *that* was the main deterrent for him to be seen by other specialities. He *had* to be seen by the mental health practitioners, no matter what.

So, a whole year went by before he was seen again, and during this time, obviously, his condition progressively worsened. During this period of time, his obsessive drinking degenerated into a whole series of different antisocial behaviours.

He developed a voracious appetite, with an obsessive impulsiveness to eat anything at hand, at tremendous speed, as if he hadn't eaten for weeks. Eating in the supermarket before reaching the checkout till became common. Sometimes he would finish eating a whole bag of donuts or a whole box of chocolates before reaching the checkout. He developed a predilection for sweets – a characteristic of the condition he unknowingly had. There was no way of going out for lunch or dinner with him, as he would devour the food and drink before everyone else and then wanted more. At home, the refrigerator was never full; he would eat absolutely anything available to him, on a daily basis. He quickly scuffled up every and any leftovers from breakfast, lunch and dinner at home. His hunger and thirst were simply insatiable.

In addition to this, he started smoking in the most compulsive way. He was capable of chain smoking an entire packet of cigarettes in under an hour. And when there were no more cigarettes, he would go outside and search for them on the street, picking up any half-smoked butt and smoking it energetically. When that option failed, he would ask random pedestrians for a cigarette, and if they weren't compliant, he would follow them to their house or to the first building they entered and wait for them outside, stalking them as he waited for the next opportunity to ask for a cigarette.

Whilst the binge eating, drinking and smoking carried on, he also developed an obsession with washing his hands and feet, to the point of damaging his skin. However, interestingly, he stopped showering.

As anyone could foresee, George's newfound behaviour caused widespread disruption: not only did he lose his job, his drivers' licence and his girlfriend but also his parents and siblings were deeply suffering as they witnessed the ongoing downward spiral he was in, without being able to do anything about it.

After about a year, his speech started to deteriorate. He went from speaking normally, to using only a few words, which he used repetitively during every 'conversation' he was engaged in. However, very interestingly, if pressed to use different words, he could. He was painfully aware of this transformation, yet he had severe difficulties expressing it. He was a prisoner of his own pain, unable to verbalise it. Interestingly, his memory – another cognitive function – was preserved for both short term and long term.

Time kept passing by and still, no one had assessed him. His family, desperate at this point, went to his GP, who took great interest in this case. He tested George for conditions such as diabetes, hypothyroidism, vitamin deficiencies, liver, kidney and electrolyte dysfunctions, infections and hormone imbalances, but all was normal, providing no helpful clues towards his diagnosis.

At this point, we reach the day of his assessment in my clinic, when his parents explained the last two years of his problems. By that time, having in hand the blood results and CT scans, I already knew a great deal about the things that George *did not* have, but I still didn't know what he *did* have.

Based on the clinical presentation, I suspected that he might have some rare form of dementia, but it seemed like a remote possibility, given his young age. More so, the CT scan of the brain he had in the past was apparently 'normal', and in dementia, one should expect to see changes on the CT scan. Nevertheless, I told them that we should do an MRI of his brain, because it was much more helpful than a plain CT scan.

The MRI proved to be very helpful. It unveiled the most likely problem that was leading to George's symptoms: extensive shrinkage of the brain tissue, specifically in the frontal and temporal lobes, bilaterally. This is usually seen in older patients who have dementia. But could this actually be dementia? Especially, considering that he was only 26 years old? Based on the cumulative results and the progressive nature of his symptoms, the answer was 'yes'!

But of course, at this stage everything was still hypothetical. In order to ground the diagnosis, he underwent specialised cognitive assessments, which revealed a specific pattern that correlated with his clinical condition. Unfortunately, the most likely diagnosis was a rare type of dementia called Frontal-Temporal Lobe Dementia (FTLD), which, as the name implies, affects mainly the frontal and the temporal lobes of the brain. More specifically, he had the 'behavioural variant' of FTLD or bvFTLD (there are another two other variants: 'semantic' FTLD or svFTLD, in which the patient loses the ability to understand or to formulate words in a spoken sentence, and 'non-fluent' or 'agrammatic' FTLD or nfFTLD, in which the patient's speech is hesitant, laboured or ungrammatical).

The reader might be wondering how he can have dementia 'without' memory loss. Essentially, FTLDs do not cause memory loss as opposed to other forms of dementia, such as Alzheimer's disease, in which there is a selective loss of short-term memories but with preserved long-term memories. The latter is usually diagnosed in the elderly, and although it can course with behavioural problems, these tend to occur late in the disease and not so early, as in FTLD.

Fortunately, these types of dementias are very rare. However, when they occur, they are devastating, not only for the patient but for the whole family. Since 2013, when I first started practising medicine in the UK, I've seen five other cases of bvFTLD (21, 26, 28, 34, and 51 years old), only one case of svFTLD and one case of nfFTLD.

The svFTLD patient arrived at my clinic after several episodes of being caught crossing the roads whilst the stop sign was on green! Essentially, he had 'lost the concept' of fear. The nfFTLD patient was a 40-year-old man who had progressively lost the ability to speak within eight months of onset.

When I told George (who unfortunately wasn't able to understand me) and his family what the diagnosis was and what type of prognosis it carried, obviously, it came as a tremendous blow. They were expecting something bad but not this bad. It was an irreversible, rapidly progressive and ultimately, lethal condition. There was no curative treatment, only symptomatic management.

As if this wasn't enough bad news, I had to tell the family that some patients with bvFTLD can carry a specific gene mutation (c9orf72) that leads to the development of Motor Neuron Disease (MND), an invariably lethal disease (Amyotrophic Lateral Sclerosis or ALS, the prototypical MND subtype, has a roughly 1000-day of life expectancy from the onset). In reality, I knew that George wouldn't be able to consent for genetic testing, but I had to tell them anyways, just in case he started to develop MND-like symptoms – mainly, progressive weakness, swallowing difficulties and shortness of breath.

Unfortunately, after about four months, he started to develop generalised weakness and wasting of all four limbs, associated with recurrent choking episodes, indicative of a difficulty to swallow. By that time, he was already living in a nursing home, requiring 24-hour supervision and assistance for all activities. Sadly, about one month later, due to an episode of aspiration pneumonia, he developed sepsis and passed away.

In such tragic cases, it's important to think about the positive things as well, even though they might seem non-existent. First of all, we were able to obtain a formal diagnosis. The reader might not think that this is not a 'positive' aspect, given the fact that the diagnosis was so devastating, but in reality, it's incredibly important because without it, George and his family would have suffered without knowing exactly why. Knowing that George's' conditions were genetic and therefore, unavoidable, gave them the peace of mind that it was completely out of their hands and that no one had done anything wrong that could have led to this. Sadly, many patients sometimes blame themselves or a family member for the conditions they have. This usually happens because of misinformation or gaps in the knowledge regarding their disease. Being able to provide a final diagnosis provides the patient and the family with a 'reason' or a 'cause', which avoids misinterpretations or suppositions that only lead to anger, sadness and an inability to move on.

A major part of obtaining a diagnosis was being able to obtain an MRI. Had George been in Peru, admitted in a government-funded or social security hospital, I can almost guarantee that this wouldn't have happened. Needless to say, there would have been no chances of doing any sort of genetic testing either.

Another positive aspect worth mentioning is that in the UK, we have world-experts that lead major research efforts into rare conditions such as FTLD. Having access to these professionals through the NHS, is truly a privilege.

The final and most important positive aspect in this case is the social assistance that George and his family received. I have never seen such a robust and generous support network as that offered by the NHS; it's truly remarkable. In Peru, George would have been forced to go back home without any assistance, and his family would have had to cope with the situation on their own. In Spain, he probably would have accessed a few community services but not the wide array that is offered in the UK. The NHS is the most vivid proof that excellent health care should and can be granted to all. Health care is a 'universal right' for all and not just a luxury for a few.

In my humble opinion, the most important duty a human being has is to take care of those who cannot take care of themselves. Governments have the responsibility of caring for their citizens. No matter how much money and success a country might have, if its citizens are not properly taken care of, the government has failed them. I have lived in four different countries – North America, Peru, Spain and UK – and I can confidently say that in the UK, there is an extremely high commitment for its citizens' wellbeing. It's a privilege to work as a consultant neurologist in the NHS, and in particular, in the James Paget University Hospital

Iris

It was such a pleasure meeting Iris with her husband. She was a wonderful 91-year-old lady, who had been married to her husband Albert for almost 60 years. She was very small, not more than five feet tall and no more than 50 kgs. So small in fact that the wheelchair she was in seemed to swallow her up completely. Albert, on the other hand, although he was also 91 years old, appeared to be slightly stronger and in overall better health conditions.

Once we were all settled in the clinic room, I asked her a little bit about the symptoms for which she had been referred to me: tremor, instability and slowness. Her GP was concerned that she might have developed Parkinson's disease.

"Well," she said, "I don't think I have Parkinson's. I think I'm just old!" She did have a valid point! As I told her, not everyone with shakes, lack of balance and slowness have Parkinson's. In fact, the older we get, the more common these symptoms become without necessarily having Parkinson's disease. Nevertheless, I wanted to make sure that I wasn't missing anything important and so asked her to lie down on the bed and to remove her clothes so that I could examine her. I left the room for a moment so that the health care assistant (HCA) could help her get undressed and lie on the bed.

When I came back, I noticed that the HCA's facial expression had changed and I really couldn't understand why. *That's strange,* I thought, but didn't make much of it. However, as soon as I focused my eyes on her right forearm, my facial expression changed as well! 'E4943' was tattooed on her forearm. Iris, noticing my state of shock, and said, "I was in Buchenwald for three years. In fact, that's where I first met Adam. We got married after the war."

Have you ever found yourself completely speechless but full of things you want to say? Well, that was how I felt at that precise moment. I felt such an honour to be standing in front of two survivors of the Holocaust, and at the same time, I felt embarrassed for not having showed them more reverence from the beginning.

Even though I wanted to ask them both a thousand questions, I had to focus on her examination. So, pretending as if 'nothing had happened', I started to examine her. Indeed, her GP was correct; she had plenty of very subtle findings in keeping with Parkinson's disease. It wasn't just age related, as Iris had assumed. However, I was pretty confident that with a small dose of medication, she would significantly improve.

Iris was unaffected by the diagnosis. So was Adam. Why would they, after all? They both had survived the worse type of atrocities imaginable with enviable courage and determination. Even at the age of 91, they both seemed able to overcome anything. Parkinson's wasn't going to be the end of Iris, and she knew it. She had literally *no fear* and that was palpable. She had lost her fear in Buchenwald. Adam had also left it behind, deeply submerged in the muddy dirt of that infernal concentration camp.

There were so many things to admire. Looking at them, speaking to them and listening to their every word was an absolute pleasure. I didn't want the appointment to end. Just thinking about what they must have gone through was overwhelming.

The only time I had witnessed another Holocaust survivor was in Lima. There was a very elderly lady who had been in Auschwitz for about two years and had managed to miraculously survive. Sadly, she had developed Alzheimer's disease and the only memories she had left were those of Auschwitz. She was incapable of forming new – nicer – memories. Alas, despite this, she always managed to smile.

In Spain, I had come across Fatima, another innocent prisoner of human stupidity and cruelty. Even though her situation wasn't as terrible as Iris's, it was nevertheless, reprehensible.

When you work in health care – in any capacity – you are given the privilege of entering other people's lives. When you step into a patient's private world, not only will you learn about the brighter side of their lives but also you will learn about their misfortunes, which, many times, are heart breaking. You are not there to pass judgement; you are there to listen, help and respect their individuality. And if you're sufficiently observant, by analysing only one patient, you will, most likely, be able to understand the actions, thoughts, behaviours, virtues and faults of those that surround him or her, because, after all, we are all the product of our environments. Listening to Iris and Adam not only told me about who they were but also who they had been, who they had become and how their environments have influenced them.

Medical school teaches you none of this. This comes from the school of life. Studying medicine is one thing but practising it is another. *Studying it requires a great deal of determination and passion but practising it requires humanity and humility. We study the science of medicine and practise the art of humaneness.*

Steve

"No matter how hard I try, I can't remember anything that happens in my day beyond 30 to 40 minutes. I can perfectly remember everything from my childhood, my best friends, where I grew up, but it's impossible for me to remember the people I've spoken to, the things that I've done, the food that I've eaten, etc., after only half an hour. It's as if I live in the past."

This was how Steve described his problem one Monday morning in clinic, as he sat next to his mum, who was clearly suffering for her eldest son.

Steve had been admitted to the hospital about a year ago with a diagnosis of viral encephalitis. And although after four weeks he had fully recovered from a physical point of view, he had been left with a permanent scar in the part of the brain that controls short-term memory: the hippocampus, which is located in the most interior portions of the temporal lobes (on the sides of the brain). This lesion had altered his life forever. He would never get it back.

Interestingly, however, he was completely able to recognise faces, even if he had seen them hours before. And this was because face recognition is processed on the most lateral parts of the temporal lobe, which weren't affected in his case. He only had damage in the most interior portions. Hence, there was a selective preservation for face recognition. In other words, he could remember who spoke to him but just not what they had said or done.

The implications of this infection were extensive. Steve went from living on his own with a stable partner, working full time and having a very active social life to breaking up with his partner, moving back in with his mother and not being able to work. Furthermore, he had to give up his driver's licence. All this happened over a period of only one month. His life was turned upside down or as he put it, 'his life had gone backwards'.

He was aware of his memory limitations. He was conscious of the fact that no matter how hard he tried he could never remember anything that had happened to him recently. He was in a perpetual state of amnesia. That's what stopped him from learning how do to new things and for that matter, to re-learn the forgotten ones. He was incapable to incorporating new information and therefore creating long-term memories. He lived in the past with only a fleeting glimpse of the present. That was it.

The pain his mum felt was palpable, the type you could only imagine yet not describe. She completed his sentences and complemented his ideas. She had become his present and his future, for he was only aware of his past. She had become his short-term memory and the sole enabler of his future. Steve was well aware of this, and it deeply affected him.

This co-dependence was both painful to witness and yet tremendously touching. She had become a widow recently, and he lost his short-term memory. *He became her company, and she became his memory.* Together they learned how to

163

survive, help each other and move through life with courage and hope.

At one point, in a joking manner – as if she desperately wanted to find something to laugh at – she said one day, "I hope I don't get Alzheimer's! Then we'll really be in trouble!" We all laughed for a moment, but I know that deep inside, it was a serious concern of hers. She was, after all, almost 80 years old.

In *Filocognicion*, a book I wrote 15 years ago, in the middle of my neurology training, I discussed the irreplaceable value of memory. After seeing many patients in Peru with acute and chronic memory loss, it became obvious to me that memory is the most important aspect of our identities. Whatever we don't remember, although it might have happened in reality, doesn't exist for us. It can't exist for us. It's as if it never happened. We live through our memories. In my opinion, losing your memory is even more impactful than losing one of your senses, simply because there's no compensatory mechanism for amnesia; there's no alternative 'method' – like braille in blindness or hearing aids in deafness – that will help (re)generate memories. Even if there's someone who can remind us of a particular event or person, without the capacity to remember, it simply 'won't exist' for us.

I had another patient who was a 24-year-old lady with diabetes type 1 (insulin-dependent diabetes), who suffered a devastating bilateral hippocampal damage due to poorly controlled diabetes and as a consequence developed severe short-term memory loss. It was so severe that she was simply unable to remember to inject herself with insulin.

Neurology is a beautiful speciality, with a rich history and an even more brilliant future. However, very sadly, for the majority of conditions, there is little treatment to offer. Loss of memory, for example, has no remedy. In fact, the majority of lesions causing some sort of sensory or cognitive loss have no treatment at all. There's 'management', at best, but certainly no treatment. This void is one of the major present-day difficulties in neurology. When I assess a patient with memory loss, it pains me to not have anything to offer. I sincerely hope that one day, neurologists can offer a satisfactory treatment for such devastating problems.